PARENTING IN THE AGE OF **SEXPOSURE**

Vandita Dubey is a Clinical Psychologist who has worked with children and families since 1995, when she joined the MA in Social Work programme at the Tata Institute of Social Sciences, Mumbai. She subsequently completed her Doctorate in Clinical Psychology in 2006 from the US. She has researched and raised awareness regarding child sexual abuse. She has also practised psychotherapy, and consulted with schools in the US and India. After seven years in Gurgaon, she chose to move to Kumaon region in the Himalayas to enjoy a simpler life, trail runs and long walks. She continues to practise and live there with her husband, two children and a dog.

PARENTING IN THE AGE OF SEXPOSURE

Raising the Precocious Generation

DR VANDITA DUBEY

RUPA

Published by
Rupa Publications India Pvt. Ltd 2016
7/16, Ansari Road, Daryaganj
New Delhi 110002

Sales centres:
Allahabad Bengaluru Chennai
Hyderabad Jaipur Kathmandu
Kolkata Mumbai

Copyright © Vandita Dubey 2016

The views and opinions expressed in this book are the author's own
and the facts are as reported by her which have been verified
to the extent possible, and the publishers are not in
any way liable for the same.

Names of some people have been changed to protect their privacy.

All rights reserved.
No part of this publication may be reproduced, transmitted, or stored in
a retrieval system, in any form or by any means, electronic,
mechanical, photocopying, recording or otherwise,
without the prior permission of the publisher.

ISBN: 978-81-291-3961-0

First impression 2016

10 9 8 7 6 5 4 3 2 1

The moral right of the author has been asserted.

Typeset by SÜRYA, New Delhi
Printed in India at Nutech Print Services, Faridabad

This book is sold subject to the condition that it shall not,
by way of trade or otherwise, be lent, resold, hired out, or otherwise
circulated, without the publisher's prior consent, in any form of
binding or cover other than that in which it is published.

For,
Raahat—my life, Anhad—my soul,
Chetan—my love

CONTENTS

Introduction	1
1. The Biological Underpinnings	4
2. Touching Genitals: What is Normal and What is Not?	16
3. The Different Expressions of Gender and Sexuality	31
4. Pitfalls and Perils of the Internet	53
5. Impact of a Highly Sexualized World: Hyper-sexuality and Body Image Concerns	66
6. Child Sexual Abuse	84
7. What Parents Can Do	105
8. Investing in a Future Free of Sexual Violence	125
Conclusion: Moral of the Story	141
References	146
Acknowledgements	165

INTRODUCTION

*To parents of infants and toddlers, their children's sexual
development may seem a long way off. But actually, sexual
development begins in a child's very first years. Infants, toddlers,
preschoolers, and young school-aged kids develop an emotional and
physical foundation for sexuality in many subtle ways as they grow.*
—KidsHealth

If you have picked up this book, you are probably a parent or someone who is concerned about children. Whoever you are, welcome to the world of adults who worry about the influences our children are growing up with, and the impact the current environment has on a child's overall development. This book is an outcome of the questions and concerns that parents in India are raising. It attempts to provide some understanding of and suggestions on how to deal with some of the issues of sex and sexuality that parents of children from birth to the age of eighteen are faced with.

So, if you are a parent who has ever asked any of the following questions, you may find some helpful information in this book:

- Are toddlers and young children sexual beings?
- When does a child's sexual development begin?
- What are the changes that a child undergoes during his/her sexual development?
- What kinds of sexual behaviour are 'normal', and what are not, for different ages?
- How does one talk to a child about sex and sexuality?
- When is a good time to talk to children about sex and sexuality?

- How can I protect my child from sexual abuse?
- How does one know if a child or adult is a child sexual abuser?
- How can I prevent my child from engaging in early sexual activity?
- How does the media bombardment of sexual information affect my child?
- How do I protect my child from the negative effects of media-fed sexualization?
- My son is interested in boys/my daughter is interested in girls. Is this behaviour normal? How should I deal with it?
- My child's behaviour does not match with his/her gender. Is there something wrong with that? How should I deal with it?
- How can I protect my child from sexual violence, in general?
- How can I help my son/daughter develop a healthy body image?
- My child is obsessed with her/his weight and looks. How should I deal with this?
- Does my child have an eating disorder?
- My child uses the Internet a lot. What are the potential dangers of the Internet?
- How should I keep my child safe from Internet dangers?

The information and suggestions in this book are based on current scientific research, theory and practice in the areas of gender and sexual development as they relate to children. In addition, I have also dipped into my own experiences and understanding developed over the past twenty years of training and working with children, parents and organizations that work with children and teenagers in India and the US.

Introduction

Studies and academic work in India on the topics discussed in this book are quite limited. Therefore, wherever possible, I have used examples from the Indian media and my practice as well as data from Indian studies. To a large extent, though, I have relied on research from the West, especially the US, where a lot of work has been done in these areas. I believe many of the concepts and research from the West are as applicable there as they are here, because of the commonalities in human experience across cultures.

Moreover, we do live in what has been called a 'global village'. The Internet, television, films, video games and music instantly and constantly subject our children to the same information and experiences that children anywhere in the world are exposed to. In addition, an increase in the mobility of families, who not only live and travel across cities in India but also across cities in different countries, has resulted in our children being exposed to varied thoughts and behaviour from different cultures. Therefore, we cannot restrict our search for answers to challenges arising out of this global exposure.

So, go ahead and explore this book. You can read it from beginning to end, or use it as a reference and read only the chapters or sections that you find pertinent. If you have very young children, I would recommend that you read the entire book. As you have probably heard countless times, 'forewarned is forearmed'! I believe knowing what to expect helps parents to be better prepared for the different developmental stages that a child will go through and the potential challenges or issues he/she might face.

Chapter 1
THE BIOLOGICAL UNDERPINNINGS

*Although I'm only fourteen, I know quite well what I want,
I know who is right and who is wrong. I have my opinions,
my own ideas and principles, and although it may sound
pretty mad from an adolescent, I feel more of a person than a child,
I feel quite independent of anyone.*
—Anne Frank

The story of our sexual development begins biologically at the time of conception, when the sperm fertilizes the ovum and we inherit a set of genes from our parents. Under normal circumstances, when one inherits two X chromosomes, one is born a female, and when one inherits one X and one Y chromosome, one is born a male. At conception there is no difference, but at around six to seven weeks of gestation, the Y chromosome becomes active and testes are formed in male foetuses. At about nine weeks of gestation, the reproductive tract and genitals are formed. At this stage, there are some differences in physiology and the type/level of hormones that circulate within male and female foetuses, which have an impact on development. In late infancy and early childhood, however, these hormones and steroids become dormant. These become active again only at the onset of puberty.[1] The adolescent years, in a way, form the second significant phase of sexual development.

In the life of a human being, at no other time does biology have as profound an impact on the human experience as it does during adolescence. However, adolescence does not occur suddenly. As a parent, you would have already noticed that the physical development of children is a process that occurs in a gradual, steady manner. From a stage when babies cannot even support their own necks to sitting up, crawling and then walking, running, climbing—physical development is continuous. The sexual development of children also follows a similar pattern. From a stage when boys and girls look alike to gradual changes in the physical appearance of girls versus boys, to reaching a stage when boys and girls become sexually mature is also a continuous process. The changes in physical appearance coincide or follow internal changes based mainly on changes in the body's production of hormones. Along with internal hormonal changes and external physical changes, sexual development is also marked by subtle or marked changes in behaviour, thoughts and feelings about oneself and others.

Like other aspects of physical growth that children undergo, sexual development occurs at a pace that is unique to each child. While there is an age range within which these changes typically occur for boys and girls, sometimes sexual development can get delayed, disrupted or occur earlier than expected. Therefore, some children may become sexually mature later or earlier than most others.

Puberty

A word that parents often talk about with a measure of apprehension is puberty. The scene that comes to mind for most parents is of their otherwise sweet, compliant child becoming unruly, rude, argumentative or non-communicative—all under the evil spell of their hormones. Popular culture, which includes movies and cartoons, often depicts adolescents acting in this manner.

However, research shows that hormones do not change the essential nature of a child. Hormones also do not drastically change the nature of the child's relationships. What does tend to happen, though, is that any difficulties or issues that may have already existed earlier in the parent–child relationship do get amplified.[2]

What exactly is puberty? The *Online Cambridge Dictionary* defines puberty as 'the stage in a person's life when they develop from a child into an adult because of changes in their body that make them able to have children'.[3] While puberty does involve maturation of the reproductive system, it is actually quite a profound process of change. The anatomical and physiological changes that occur during puberty alter not only the way children look but also the way they feel and think about themselves and how they relate to others. Thus, changes occur at a physical, emotional, social and sexual level.

Brain research shows that the human brain continues to grow and does not attain full maturity until the early twenties.[4] The adolescent brain, while as intellectually capable as an adult's brain, does not function in the same way as an adult's brain. Research shows that adolescents are more tuned in emotionally than children or adults. At the same time, impulse control is not developed.[5] Hence, while teenagers know about safe, unsafe or risky behaviour intellectually, and are very capable of understanding situations hypothetically and giving the 'right' answers, their impulse control does not work as well when actually faced with a situation that might put them at risk.[6] Therefore, they are very likely to engage in risky behaviour. Alcohol, drugs and nicotine have a greater addictive potential for the still developing adolescent brain.[7] New studies suggest that puberty, and not age, is related to sensation-seeking, drug use and emotional reactivity.[8]

At the same time, development during puberty is not uniform—a child may grow within the physical parameters of puberty, but may not mature emotionally or socially at the same rate. How an adolescent behaves is determined by many factors, including socio-cultural or environmental, genetic and psychological factors that are specific to him or her.[9]

The mechanics of puberty

While talking about puberty, it is important to first understand the physical and physiological changes that a child undergoes during this phase. Boys and girls undergo a series of changes that are triggered by sex hormones.

On one random, insignificant night in the child's life, a part of the brain called the hypothalamus begins to release the gonadotrophin-releasing hormone. In the beginning, this hormone is released in small amounts periodically. Over some days, however, it becomes a steady, consistent stream. It then stimulates the pituitary gland to start producing the follicle-stimulating hormone and luteinizing hormone, which travel to the testes of boys and ovaries of girls and bring about the physical changes associated with puberty. After some time, girls' ovaries start producing oestrogen and progesterone and boys' testes begin to produce testosterone, which further fuel changes culminating in girls having their first periods and boys experiencing their first ejaculation.[10]

This is a phase of development during which the child's hormones cause internal and external changes in the child's body, which the child can neither predict nor control. All these changes have a significant impact on a child's mood and it may seem as if the child is often over-reacting to situations.

The following facts—in rough timelines—chart the changes that your child will undergo during puberty.[11] While looking at these timelines, it is important to remember that each child is different and the age at which puberty begins varies from one child to another.

Pubertal changes in girls

- The normal age range for girls to enter puberty is eight to thirteen years and puberty typically ends by fourteen–fifteen years.
- It takes about two years from the time puberty begins to the time it ends. However, the duration of puberty may be shorter or longer for different children.
- On an average, puberty in girls begins at age eleven with breast growth, appearance of pubic hair and development of the womb, along with 7–8 cms of annual height gain.
- In the following year, around age twelve, height gain is maximum at approximately 8 cms. Acne on the face and back may appear and underarm hair begins to grow.
- In the following year, around age thirteen, height gain slows down. Menstruation typically occurs two years after breast growth has started and is, therefore, likely to begin at this age. Periods may be irregular initially but usually within six to twelve months of the first menstrual bleeding, periods become more regular.
- Height gain in girls ends within one to two years of the first period. Puberty ends when girls attain the physical appearance of mature female adults with fully developed genitals. This stage occurs around fourteen–fifteen years of age.

Pubertal changes in boys

- Puberty in boys can begin any time between the ages of nine and fourteen. On an average, though, puberty in boys

begins around age twelve with physical changes of the scrotum and testicles and appearance of pubic hair.
- During the following year, around age thirteen, the penis and testicles undergo growth. About a third of teenage boys may also experience minor growth in breast tissue, which settles down after a few years. Boys at this age may experience 'wet dreams' or involuntary ejaculation of semen during sleep. The voice usually 'breaks', that is, the tone and pitch of voice varies for short periods of time. The size of muscles usually increases and a gain in height of about 7–8 cms occurs.
- Growth continues throughout the following year. There is further growth of the penis and testicles and appearance of underarm hair. The voice tends to change permanently and some boys may develop acne.
- Around age fifteen, facial hair may begin to grow and some boys may start shaving. Boys' genitals at this age begin to look like that of adult males. Gain in height may slow down and boys usually stop growing around age sixteen. However, muscular growth may still continue.
- Most boys attain full physical maturity by age eighteen.

Delayed puberty

Sometimes, puberty can be delayed in both boys and girls. Puberty in boys is delayed mainly due to physical or physiological reasons. However, puberty in girls may be delayed due to either physical/physiological or psychological/environmental reasons.[12]

While medical reasons are not in a parent's control and, therefore, cannot really be prevented, the non-medical/environmental/lifestyle-related reasons are what parents can watch out for. For example, lead, the metal and an environmental pollutant, seems to affect puberty. Research has shown that girls with high levels of lead in their blood tend to experience delayed puberty.[13, 14] Puberty can also get delayed due to strict dieting to the point when anorexia nervosa, a psychological disorder, is diagnosed.[15] Anorexia is a condition that most often afflicts young girls although adult men, women and boys may also suffer from it. Anorexia is a disorder in which people restrict their diet as a way of controlling their appearance based on a distorted perception of their body. This means that people who are quite thin still see themselves as fat and restrict their diet to such an extreme that they become underweight, and sometimes have to be hospitalized for malnutrition. In some cases, people suffering from anorexia have died due to medical complications caused by anorexia.

An extreme lack of calorie consumption or a significant decrease in body fat affects the normal process of puberty.[16] Extremely taxing exercise, such as the kind of heavy training that gymnasts or athletes undergo, can cause a deficiency of calories in the body. In these cases, more calories are required by the body than are being consumed. When faced with malnutrition, the human body goes into a shut-down mode and all activities, except for those essential to survival, cease. For the human body, regardless of what the conscious human mind might say, reproduction is not essential for survival. The most common way in which a deficiency of calories affects puberty is by causing menstruation or periods to either get delayed or stop altogether. In fact, calorie deficiency can affect a woman's menstrual cycle at any age, not just the teenage years.

Precocious puberty

Puberty can sometimes occur much earlier than expected. Precocious puberty is the term used when girls show signs of entering puberty early, which is considered to be before the child is eight years old. For boys, those who appear to be entering puberty at age nine are considered to be undergoing precocious puberty.[17] Early puberty seems to be more common amongst girls but the reasons for it are not fully established. In general, puberty seems to be occurring at a younger age than it did decades ago. The risk factors identified for early puberty include changes in diet, obesity, being of a certain racial origin, for example, African-American, exposure to radiation therapy or to sex hormones via medication/ointments, some medical conditions,[18] and the presence of environmental pollutants that impact the human endocrine system.[19] Some chemicals, such as the pesticide DDT, have been banned due to this reason. Studies are still on to study the impact on puberty of other environmental pollutants, such as plastics.[20]

Precocious puberty has some potential negative consequences for children. Those undergoing precocious puberty often seem to gain height earlier than their peers but then, their growth also stops early as their bones mature earlier. Hence, children going through precocious puberty tend to be shorter than their peers.[21] It is very important for adolescents to fit in or identify with their peers. Children going through precocious puberty, however, may feel that they are different from their peers. They are likely to experience changes in their bodies and unfamiliar feelings but not be able to share these with other children. They may feel very self-conscious about their changing body and may get teased by other children who have not yet begun to go through the same changes. This may impact their self-esteem and lead to more serious mental health issues. They may also get exposed to alcohol/drug use and engage in sexual activity earlier than their peers.[22]

While, as a parent, you cannot do anything about the genetic/medical factors that cause precocious puberty, you can definitely help your child maintain a healthy weight and prevent exposure to sex hormones or other harmful chemicals. In case your child does go through precocious or early puberty, the most important thing to do is to help the child understand that puberty is a normal process and that all children, sooner or later, will go through it. Provide an opening for your children to talk about any concerns or worries they may have and continue to have conversations with them about their experience of puberty.

Talking to children about puberty

Within reasonable limits, it is never too early or too late to talk to children about their bodies and the changes they can expect to undergo or might already be undergoing. As each child undergoes puberty at a different time, it is possible that your child may not have entered puberty while his/her friends may have already begun to do so. If so, it is possible that their friends may have shared whatever information they have regarding puberty with your child. Your child's friends may have factual and correct information, or they may be misinformed. Again, their perceptions and attitudes may be coloured by their parents' perceptions and attitudes, which may or may not be a positive influence on your child. In addition, young people these days are exposed to ideas about puberty and dating from the Internet, television programmes or movies.[23]

Rather than leaving your child to form his/her perceptions and attitudes based on misinformation or other people's value systems, it is better to talk openly with your child about puberty. On an average, girls enter puberty around age ten and boys at age eleven and so, having these discussions before age ten seems to make sense. If in your family history, boys and girls have tended to enter puberty at an earlier age, it may be advisable to have these discussions perhaps as early as age eight. Your family physician or paediatrician may also be able to assess the situation and tell you if your child is likely to enter puberty early.

While puberty is a normal biological process, in India there are many practices attached to it. In some villages and among some families in urban areas, menstruation is a time when girls and women are considered unclean. Suhasini is a twenty-five-year-old well-educated professional who works in one of the largest technology firms of the country and often travels abroad for projects. She recently got married to a person whose family believes that women are unclean during their menstruation. She is, therefore, required to sleep on the floor and not practise any religious rituals during her menstrual periods. While this is a fairly common practice in villages and smaller towns in India, it may come as a shock to some urban, educated parents who may look at such practices as regressive and insulting to women. On the other hand, these practices may seem to make perfect sense to certain families. As parents, you have to decide what your outlook on this topic is going to be and communicate that to your child.

Menstruation is a special time in a young girl's life and it is very important to specifically talk to girls about menstruation before they go through it. It is one of the changes that occurs literally overnight and can trigger many emotions. If not aware and prepared for it, girls may feel frightened and anxious that they have contracted some serious illness or disorder. Shalini is a twelve-year-old who one day discovered some blood in her underclothes. She was very scared and did not tell anyone in her family as she was convinced that she had contracted a life-threatening illness. Her parents would often scold her for eating with the same spoon as her friends, and Shalini was convinced that this behaviour had caused her illness. It was only when they were travelling during her second period that her mother accidentally discovered that Shalini was menstruating and then talked to her about it.

Similarly, it is very important to talk to boys about ejaculation and involuntary ejaculation during sleep or 'wet dreams' before they experience it. Some boys may experience their first ejaculation before they have grown facial hair or begin to look older. If they are not prepared for it, experiencing ejaculation, especially 'wet dreams', may be embarrassing or overwhelming for the child. There are certain myths that also exist around ejaculation and male masturbation, such as masturbation can hurt the penis or make the person go blind. These are scientifically incorrect notions.

When talking to your child, it is important to make sure that your information is correct and that you give your children accurate, factual information. There are two reasons for this: firstly, if your information is faulty, they may look for advice from somewhere else, and from then on not believe the information you share with them; secondly, if you do not give them factual information, they may seek it from other sources and believe whatever anyone else tells them, which may be incorrect and potentially harmful for them.

The most important message that needs to be conveyed to children is that puberty is normal. You have gone through it, others have gone through it, and your child will also do so. Everyone's experiences may be slightly different and the exact age or sequence in which they experience these changes may differ a bit, but it is all normal. Puberty and all the changes associated with it—pubic hair, breaking voice, menstruation, wet dreams, confusion, increased emotionality or greater sensitivity to emotional situations, self-consciousness, focus on physical appearance, 'crushes' or sexual feelings are all part of the normal process.[24]

It is crucial to start talking to children about puberty before they enter it. A single 'birds and bees' talk does not help. Talking about puberty and the changes that the child will undergo, or is already going through, is an ongoing conversation. It is best to take up this topic in a non-formal, casual way rather than a 'let's sit and talk about it' fashion. Often broaching the topic by sharing your own experiences of puberty, whether it is menstruation or wet dreams or anything else, works well. You could say, 'When I was your age, I had my first period,' and then go on to share how you felt or experienced this change—what helped you and what did not. This helps children know that the changes they are going through and the feelings or thoughts they have about these changes are all normal. It also tells them that you are comfortable talking about this topic and that it is perfectly fine to talk about it. Once they realize that you can be approached, they are more likely to ask you for information and advice.

Provide factual information in as detailed a manner as the child wants to know. In many ways, information is power, and in this case, it also gives the child a sense of comfort and confidence. In addition, by talking to your child about puberty, you become the primary information-provider and your child is then more likely to come to you when trying to make decisions about sex, which is ultimately a parent's biggest concern.

Chapter 2

TOUCHING GENITALS: WHAT IS NORMAL AND WHAT IS NOT?

It can be hard to acknowledge that all of us, even children, are sexual beings, have sexual feelings and are curious about sex and sexuality.
—Stop It Now!

Sunita, a well-educated young professional, had come back from work after picking up her two-and-a-half-year-old daughter from play school. She sat playing with her daughter on the sofa when the doorbell rang. Two male workers had turned up at the door to fix a plumbing problem in the flat. As Sunita showed the men into the house, she noticed her daughter sitting on the sofa with her diaper off, genitals in full view, touching herself. Sunita suddenly felt a mix of emotions—embarrassment bordering on shame, discomfort, anger. She quickly directed the men towards the kitchen to fix the plumbing problem and shouted at her daughter to get off the sofa and go to her room.

Why did the two-and-a-half-year-old girl take off her diaper? Why did Sunita get so upset and shout at her? Well, Sunita's daughter did what most two-and-a-half-year-old children would do, and Sunita reacted just as many Indian women would. Children of this age touch themselves because they are curious. In fact, children from the first year of life until they are about six to seven years old touch themselves as they would touch any of their body parts because they are curious about their bodies and how they work.[1]

Touching Genitals: What Is Normal and What Is Not?

Often, around six months of age, when children start sitting up unassisted and begin to crawl, they can easily reach their genitals and will often touch them. This behaviour occurs in full public view and continues until parents or other adults tell them not to touch themselves in public. Boys often discover around this time that the penis undergoes changes in response to their touch. However, even at this time, touching is not sexual in the way it is for adults. It is all part of the curiosity that children feel.

Parents will observe that children are also fascinated with and will talk about 'potty' and 'sussu' (urination). Their conversations with each other often focus on these topics, even in public settings. This is all due to their general fascination at this age with different body parts and their functions.[2]

The important thing to remember is that preschool age children do not have emotions attached to any body part. They feel neither embarrassed to show them nor shy about talking about their body parts, including their genitals.[3] However, the adults around them often have many different emotions attached to talking about genitals.

How an adult addresses the child's behaviour of exposing himself/herself or touching his/her own genitals forms the first piece of communication related to the child's perception of his/her own body.[4] How one perceives or thinks about one's body is very important as it forms the foundation for one's comfort or discomfort with one's sexuality as an adult. Hence, when adults use reprimands like 'shame, shame, cover yourself up' or 'yuck, what are you doing!' it communicates a message to the child that their genitals and anything to do with them needs to be hidden and/or to feel ashamed of. It communicates that genitals are in some way 'dirty', so children learn to associate guilt with touching their own genitals and with feeling good due to this touch.

If a negative attitude towards the body persists, it often causes problems in adult marital/romantic relationships because of the discomfort with one's body and sex. More immediately, it also causes children to hide any questions they may have about sex and sexuality or to seek out information from people other than their parents. Mostly, the people they turn to then are other children who often do not have complete or correct information, or they turn to the Internet which can further put them at risk.[5]

While children, from infants to four-year-olds, initially touch their genitals out of curiosity, it also happens that they find the act of touching or rubbing their genitals soothing or pleasurable. It is in this way that children often discover 'masturbation'. The online psychology dictionary defines masturbation as the process of manipulating one's own genital organs, whether a penis or clitoris, for the purposes of self-stimulating, which does not require a partner.[6] However, masturbation as displayed by children is mostly not pleasurable in the same way that it may be for adults.

Young children do not have the sexual drive or surge of hormones that is the basis for sexual behaviour, including masturbation, in teenagers and adults.[7] Sometimes, young children tend to touch, stroke or play with their genitals when they are bored, sleepy or watching television.[8] If they do manipulate their genitals at other times of the day in public or at preschool, they can easily be distracted. Sometimes, giving the child extra hugs can take away his/her need to get physical comfort or be soothed through touching his/her genitals.

Mental health professionals recommend that the child's behaviour of touching his/her own genitals, which is referred to as masturbation (though it is different from masturbation the way adolescents and adults engage in it), should be handled in such a manner that no negative emotions are attached to it. The best way to do so is to tell the child in a gentle and matter-of-fact manner that they can touch themselves but only in the privacy of their bathroom or bedroom, not in public.[9] This message like most instructions about cleanliness and good habits, 'do nots' such as not picking their nose or washing hands before eating, will have to be repeated many times over. Most children, over time, understand and stop engaging in such behaviour in public.

It is important to remember that children are in no way harming themselves physically or psychologically by touching themselves or by masturbating. Masturbation does not result in any immediate or long-term harm to the child. This behaviour is normal and natural and does not need to be stopped as long as the child displays no anxiety about it or is not preoccupied by it to the exclusion of other childhood interests and activities.[10]

Children are social beings, which means that they are also curious about other people and that includes other children and adults. Therefore, the curiosity that children display towards their own bodies extends to the bodies of others.[11] If children have siblings at home, they may have seen the genitals of the opposite sex, but if they have not, then this exposure usually occurs during preschool or early school years. At this stage, children have common washrooms at school and they notice that their genitals are different from that of the opposite sex.

Children often ask parents why their genitals look different from that of the opposite sex. You may also find that your daughter insists on not sitting on the pot and instead urinates standing because she has seen her older brother do that. On the other hand, unless shown how to by their father/older brother, boys may continue to sit and urinate like they have seen their mothers do. The best way to deal with the difference question is to say that boys and girls are different, and so, their genitals are not alike. Neither sex is better than the other, they are just not the same in bodily features, which is why they find different ways of using the toilet more convenient/easy.

Often, children will want to see what adult bodies look like.[12] Younger children may touch women's breasts out of curiosity or want to see how their parents bathe or use the toilet. As one teaches the child names for various body parts, one can also start the conversation saying that genitals are private and that underwear keeps private areas covered. At a very young age, children may not understand the concept of privacy but gradually, around the age of four to six years, they begin to understand and implement it, enforcing it for themselves.[13] It is important to not scold young children and be more accepting of their nudity as that is what comes naturally to them.[14] Though they are still curious, they learn that other children and adults need privacy, too, and to respect this.

When it comes to touching others, especially other children, one needs to handle the issue in a somewhat different manner. Childhood games, such as 'Doctor, doctor' or 'Show me yours and I'll show you mine', have been played by children all over the world over for decades. These games are also a part of the normal, natural curiosity that children have about the bodies of others. As long as these games are played openly between children of the same age and developmental level, and children stop playing such games when asked to, there is nothing to worry about. Normally, one can intervene in children's mutual exploratory games by reiterating that genitals are private and they should not touch each other's genitals—again in a calm, matter-of-fact manner.[15]

These games can be signals of more serious problems, however, if they involve pressurizing or forcing another child to

Touching Genitals: What Is Normal and What Is Not?

play such games, imitating sexual intercourse, inserting objects into genitals, touching the genitals of another child, being secretive about such games or continuing to play them even when asked to stop. In case you notice any such behaviour, it is best to stop the activity and ask the children involved where they had seen or experienced such behaviour. These behaviours can result from sexual abuse, from accidentally witnessing adults engage in sexual activity, or arise due to other psychological issues. You may need to inform the parents of the children concerned about it and contact a mental health professional who is trained and experienced in handling such matters.[16]

Most children between the ages of four and six, who have been explained that genitals and masturbation are private, are often mindful of their own and other people's privacy and may not engage in such games to begin with. Hence, it makes sense to start communicating this idea to children from an early age—it in no way harms and can only benefit the child and others. However, there will be children who will try to peep in when their friends are using the washroom or sometimes even try to pull each other's pants down. This behaviour needs to be dealt with by firmly and calmly telling the child that it is inappropriate to peep in or pull at someone's clothes, or do anything that the other child does not want. It is a general message of respecting other people's space, no matter whether the other child is a boy or girl.

Once children start speaking, they ask many questions. They notice that the adult male and female body look different. Children between four to six years may point to a woman's breasts and ask what they are. They may be curious about women's underclothes. Or they may want to know why men have more body hair or why they do not have breasts.[17] With questions like these, it is best to be factual and use appropriate words for parts of the body—do not use slang words.[18] Hence, you can simply tell the child that women have breasts. If they have been touching someone's breasts, you can add that it is a private area and it is not appropriate to touch them.

Children around this age also begin to ask where babies come from. Often, children who live in big cities see food, toiletries and other items come from the market and may think babies also come from a shop. Ravi, an inquisitive five-year-old, would often ask his mother which shop she had bought him from. Or if a relative has had a baby at a hospital, they may think babies are available at hospitals. The best way to address such questions is to be factual and to provide short, simple answers. Ravi's mother explained that babies do not come from shops, they are born. She told him that he was born from her tummy and added that all babies are born from their mother's tummy. Usually, such an answer is enough to satisfy a child of Ravi's age. There is no need for a more detailed explanation.

Rahul is a six-year-old boy who, while travelling on the train with his mother, went into the washroom with her. Rahul's mother was menstruating and he happened to catch a glimpse of her adjusting her sanitary napkin. Rahul came out of the washroom convinced that his mother used diapers and promptly told his best friend at school the next day that his mother wore diapers! Often, it is best to ignore such a conversation between children. It is often a temporary topic of conversation which is soon forgotten.

However, topics that keep recurring or questions that are asked often need to be addressed or answered in a short simple way.[19] The key is to stick to the question being asked. Most parents avoid or dread children's questions because they assume they will need to give lengthy, detailed answers, but the rule of thumb is to stick to answering the specific question that the child has asked with a short-sentence answer, which does not include statements such as 'You're too young, you won't understand' or 'I'll tell you when you grow up'. These evasive responses just increase the curiosity of children since they never believe they will not be able to understand. They will just stop asking you and ask their best friend, or anyone else who is willing to give them an answer, instead!

Children in the age group of four to six years are exposed to adult behaviour either directly or indirectly via movies and television programmes. Kissing on the mouth is often shown as part of romantic scenes, even in cartoon movies meant for children. For example, most Disney movies like *Frozen* show characters kissing on the mouth. Children at this age may also witness more intimate scenes because of media exposure. Accidentally, they may even have seen adults engage in such behaviour.

While children at this age may not understand anything about such displays, they will imitate them, not being able to judge whether such behaviour is appropriate or not.[20] They tend to imitate whatever they observe adults or older children doing. Again, different strategies work in such a situation. The most important thing is to not react with strong emotions, whether embarrassment or anger. Or even if you do feel these emotions, it is important not to show them and try to stay calm.

Ignoring often works, as children will usually imitate a behaviour but then forget it and get involved in other childhood activities. This is because it really does not have any relevance in their life, other childhood activities being more meaningful for them. At other times, distraction may be in order and it works quite well too, mostly for the same reason. If you do have to intervene, provide an explanation that makes sense to them, such as saying that kissing on the mouth is not ideal because germs can be passed on.

Children of this age also like to use words that are considered forbidden or 'naughty'. These include slang or curse words they may have heard, or just about any words they think will get a reaction from adults.[21] Children, often, do not know or understand what these words mean—all they know is that certain words usually evoke emotion in adults and help attract their attention. Often, the best way to deal with the use of inappropriate words is to ignore the child since the more one reacts, the more the child is likely to use the word.

With older children one can also explain that such words are rude—but the caveat is that one needs to be careful not to use these words oneself. Or on the rare occasion that you happen to use such a word involuntarily, say, for example, it was because a hammer fell on your toe. Apologizing to the child for using it, and reiterating that it is not a nice word, often works. What usually does not work is using such words oneself and then insisting that adults can use such words but children cannot. Children often do not buy the logic of 'just because I am an adult I can do this, but you cannot.' Say this and you are likely to have a rebellion on your hands!

As children grow older, their behaviour changes. Often, around the age of five to six years, children become conscious of their bodies and nudity.[22] This may sometimes happen earlier, especially if the family environment is such that privacy has been encouraged. Children then do not like it if other children or adults, other than their parents, see them naked. They start closing the bathroom door when they are bathing, changing clothes or using the toilet. If they masturbate, they begin to do so only in private.

While they are still quite curious about other people's bodies, children gradually begin to understand that other people need and expect privacy too. The next time that Rahul travelled in the train with his mother, he was seven-and-a-half years old and this time he covered his eyes, without being asked to, while his mother used the toilet.

Both masturbation, once it has begun, and curiosity about one's body continue as children grow and approach puberty. Children also continue to display a curiosity about other people's bodies. They may look at pictures of nude people and may also display curiosity about conversations pertaining to sex and sexuality.[23] Overall, though, children in the seven to ten age group are more focused on sports, friendships and academic learning.

As children enter adolescence, sexual topics gain greater prominence. Adolescence can be defined in various ways but in general, it is considered to be the period between ages ten to eighteen. The initial phase of adolescence roughly coincides with the onset of puberty. Because children enter puberty at different ages, each child also enters adolescence at a different age.

Adolescence is a phase of transition which takes the child from childhood into adulthood. It is a time when a number of changes occur around the same time. These changes impact the adolescents' physical appearance, their thinking abilities, their social interactions with adults and peers, their self-perception and their emotional life.[24]

Most parents realize their child is entering adolescence when the child begins to appear a bit moody; his/her emotions fluctuate and seem more intense than before. It may seem difficult to get compliance from an adolescent child in the same way that one did earlier, and arguments with the child become more common. Children often become more conscious of their appearance and spend considerable amounts of time and energy on how they want to look.

Socially, adolescents seem to withdraw from parents and adults in general, preferring the company of peers. Fitting in and being accepted by their peer group becomes more important than before.[25] Both boys and girls insist they need privacy and space. All these changes are normal but parents sometimes find it difficult to adapt to them. Rohini, the mother of a fourteen-year-old boy, is one such parent. Rohini often complains that her son has emotionally pushed her away. She sometimes finds it difficult to get through to her child. She misses not knowing all the tiny details of his life as she did earlier. She also craves the hugs and kisses she used to get from her son because now they are rare. Her son appears to have a girlfriend and spends large amounts of time talking to this girl over the phone.

It is crucial to remember that when your child goes through adolescence, he/she is going through a number of changes physically and psychologically.[26] Adolescents often do not understand why and how they feel the way they do. They do not always feel in control of their emotions but at the same time, they can feel a variety of complex emotions—some they have never experienced before.

A more developed cognitive ability also means that teenagers can think in very complex ways, can analyse matters and challenge what you say. Adolescents tend to be very idealistic and so are likely to question any discrepancy of thought and action that you as a parent may display.

One way to look at adolescence is that it is a time when adolescents try out their various developing abilities within the safety-net of the family. They are experimenting with and rehearsing for the emotional and cognitive independence that they are expected to display as an adult. They are trying to spread their wings and take little hops before they have the ability and confidence to fly away. The changes children go through in adolescence are an essential and natural part of growing up.

Adolescence also marks the beginning of more adult-like sexual interest and expression. Before puberty, the interest in others is mainly driven by curiosity. However, around the time of puberty, children begin to show more of an attraction or romantic interest in others.[27] They may fantasize about film stars or develop a 'crush' on actors or singers they have never met. They may begin to have 'special' friends or call such friends 'boyfriend' or 'girlfriend', but their behaviour is likely to be restricted to long conversations or for social status, that is, showing off that they are more sophisticated or 'with it' because they have a boyfriend/girlfriend. All this is normal behaviour.

Adolescents have a strong need to belong and their behaviour is often influenced by their peer group.[28] There are boys and girls who are considered 'popular' and they set the standards for what is considered 'cool'. What is considered 'cool' is also dictated in large part by what children are exposed to through various forms of media—films, songs, television programmes, books and the Internet.

At the same time, adolescents also make some complex judgement calls. They may consider what is 'cool' but may also keep in mind what the larger cultural context is, especially in terms of sexual behaviour. Children are often well aware of their family's values regarding sexuality and will often behave in accordance with what would be acceptable to the family. They may stretch the boundary a bit, but usually not very far out.

During the early years of adolescence, mutual sexual contact or sexual touching of any kind between children in India is unusual. As they grow older, however, things may begin to change. A 2012 study conducted at two schools in Pune with students from classes nine to twelve found that some boys and girls in the thirteen–fourteen age group had begun sexual contact.[29]

The sexual behaviours the researchers studied included masturbation, kissing, touching each other's private parts and sexual intercourse. What they found was that out of 586 students, 55.7 per cent of boys and 21.9 per cent of girls masturbated. However, only 30.08 per cent of the boys and 17.18 per cent of the girls engaged in sexual contact, and the average age at which they had their first sexual contact with someone, which did not include sexual intercourse, was around thirteen–fourteen years.

What this finding means is that children's interest in their peers at the age of thirteen–fourteen years acquires more of a sexual component and they are ready to experiment with 'dating' behaviours. This change in behaviour occurs as a result of, and in the context of, the physical and hormonal changes that their bodies undergo due to puberty.

When it comes to sexual intercourse, which is what a majority of parents worry about the most, the above-mentioned study reported that a much smaller percentage of those who had initiated sexual contact at thirteen–fourteen years went on to have sexual intercourse; 6.31 per cent of the boys and 1.31 per cent of the girls reported engaging in sexual intercourse for the first time at the average age of fifteen–sixteen years.

As we do not have large-scale studies from India on sexual behaviour of adolescents, we do not have a true picture of the sexual activity amongst Indian adolescents. There are bound to be differences in the way adolescents behave in rural areas versus urban areas, small towns versus metropolitan cities, and possibly across socio-economic strata and education levels as well.

The findings of this study do largely coincide with anecdotal data, which is what we know through experiences reported by young people in an informal manner. Hence, masturbation, use of pornography, holding hands, touching and kissing are more common, while touching each other's private parts and sexual intercourse are not so common at this age, especially among girls in India.

Is any of this sexual behaviour 'normal' for adolescents? Is it 'okay' for adolescents to engage in sexual behaviour of any kind, or what kind of behaviours are 'okay' and what are not? These are questions that can only be answered by individual families for themselves. When we look at the West, a very different kind of data emerges.

According to a 2007 US study[30] that looked at large-scale survey data from 1954 to 2003, the average age of first intercourse for adolescents in 2003 in the US was around seventeen years. The average age of first intercourse in the 1950s, however, was twenty and has steadily come down over the following decades. Overall, 77 per cent of the respondents were found to have had sexual intercourse by the time they turned twenty.

Hence, sexual intercourse by children in their late teens is not an exception but quite common, and premarital sex is accepted as 'normal' in the US. Researchers attribute this to the fact that both men and women in the US typically do not marry until their mid to late twenties. Delay in the marriage age is becoming a reality in India too, but acceptance of premarital sex is almost non-existent.

Hence, if a teenager aged nineteen, had sex and got pregnant, what it would look like for her would be very different, depending on where she was born. Darshini, a young nineteen-year-old who studied at a reputed Delhi school and had a steady boyfriend, was excited to go abroad for her undergraduate studies. Days before she was to fly out, she found out that she was pregnant. Scared of how her parents would react, she went around in an autorickshaw all alone, in the summer heat of Delhi, looking for a gynaecologist. She had enough money and was able to pay for a safe abortion. However, she never shared this experience with anyone. And even now after four years, she is unable to get over the fear, guilt and shame that the experience left her with.

This again brings us to what is 'normal'. What is normal is that physical and hormonal changes which occur during puberty. What is also normal is that these changes create sexual interest in adolescent boys and girls and they have the ability to engage in sexual relationships. Whether or not adolescents pursue their sexual interests, or the kind of sexual activities they engage in, are determined mainly by family values and the larger socio-cultural context regarding what is considered acceptable behaviour and what is not.

Whether adolescents have the maturity to make decisions regarding what kind of sexual activities or sexual relationships to engage in is a matter for debate. There are problems associated with engaging in sexual intercourse too early, especially if it ends up in pregnancy or exposure to sexually transmitted diseases. This is a factor that most people, whether in the West or in India, worry about.

It is a scientific fact that the brain of most people is still developing well into their twenties. What this means is that the area of the brain that is involved in long-term planning, decision-making, impulse control and making sound judgements regarding varied situations is not yet fully developed in adolescence. Hence, many adolescents tend to be impulsive risk-takers, who believe no harm will ever come to them, no matter what they do. It, therefore, makes sense to think of ways in which adults in the adolescent's life can promote the development of healthy sexuality, while also helping adolescents make sound, informed choices regarding sex.

Chapter 3

THE DIFFERENT EXPRESSIONS OF GENDER AND SEXUALITY

Whether we are straight or LGBT ourselves, parents need to be as loving as possible when our sons or daughters choose to come out to us about their sexual orientation or their gender identity. It takes courage for children to come out to their parents. When our children come out, it means that they have begun to accept themselves for who they are. It also shows that they want to have an open and honest relationship with us.
—Planned Parenthood

A generation or two ago the word 'gay' held only one meaning in India and that was 'happy'. For most parents now, especially in urban areas, 'gay' is a somewhat familiar term and is, in general, used to refer to people who are of a homosexual orientation. 'Straight', which was the quality of a line connecting two points, now refers to people who are of a heterosexual orientation. Not only have these words been given new meanings but new emotions have also been attached to them. For example, 'gay' may be a familiar term, but for many people it is not an entirely comfortable term, as across continents we still struggle to break away from old ways of thinking that view being 'gay', 'queer', 'bisexual', 'lesbian', 'transgender' as immoral, abnormal or wrong. However, all these labels stand for valid human experiences that we or our children may identify with. Let us look at some of these definitions and labels as they relate to our children's sexual development.

Sexual orientation

Sexual orientation is defined as a person's romantic or sexual interest or attraction towards another person of the opposite sex, same sex, or both the sexes. Sexual orientation can be described as heterosexual, homosexual or bisexual. According to the American Psychological Association (APA), 'Research over several decades has demonstrated that sexual orientation ranges along a continuum, from exclusive attraction to the other sex to exclusive attraction to the same sex.'[1]

The APA brochure on sexual orientation adds, 'Sexual orientation is commonly discussed as if it were solely a characteristic of an individual, like biological sex, gender identity, or age. This perspective is incomplete because sexual orientation is defined in terms of relationships with others. People express their sexual orientation through behaviours with others, including such simple actions as holding hands or kissing. Thus, sexual orientation is closely tied to the intimate personal relationships that meet deeply felt needs for love, attachment, and intimacy. In addition to sexual behaviours, these bonds include non-sexual physical affection between partners, shared goals and values, mutual support, and ongoing commitment. Therefore, sexual orientation is not merely a personal characteristic within an individual. Rather, one's sexual orientation defines the group of people in which one is likely to find the satisfying and fulfilling romantic relationships that are an essential component of personal identity for many people.[2]

'At the same time, it is important to recognize that sexual or romantic interest, and sexual expression or engaging in sexual acts, are two separate things. To put it in other words, the sexual acts that a person engages in may or may not give any information about their sexual orientation. Many adults and young people who identify themselves as gay, lesbian, or bisexual have never

The Different Expressions of Gender and Sexuality

engaged in any sexual acts with a person of the same sex. And, many people who have had same-sex experiences may not view themselves as gay, lesbian or bisexual. This fact has particular significance for parents because adolescence is a time when children first make discoveries regarding their own sexuality and may experiment with different sexual expressions.'[3]

Hence, it is wise not to jump to conclusions regarding your child's sexuality based on a specific behaviour or two.

Examples of sexual exploration and experimentation abound from studies and anecdotal evidence gathered in India, especially from boys. Sexual activity often occurs between boys. Street children as well as children from all-male boarding schools have often reported such activity. This sexual activity tends to involve an older and a younger boy where the older boy is more active, and masturbation or penetration may occur. These sexual acts may be seen by the children involved as consensual, with no force or intimidation being used. The same children as adolescents or, later, as adults may never identify themselves as homosexual or gay. They may also clearly prefer or be solely interested in females as romantic or sexual partners.

This phenomenon is generally viewed from the perspective of sexual exploration and issues of access and opportunity. It is not that these boys are sexually or romantically attracted to other boys. It is just that in the absence of access to females and/or the opportunity to explore their sexuality with females, they explore it amongst themselves. It is also important to separate such activity from instances of male child sexual abuse or rape where asserting power is the motive behind engaging in sexual acts.

On the other hand, there are countless adults who spend much of their lives in heterosexual relationships, only to discover that they are actually romantically interested in people of their own sex. One such story is that of Narendra who discovered his sexual orientation as an adult. Narendra is a forty-year-old male nurse from a small town in north India who got married in his mid-twenties. He had an arranged marriage and has two biological children. While Narendra has no complaints against his wife and thinks she is a good person, he has never felt sexually attracted to her or to any other woman. He has always found himself having sexual fantasies involving men but never acted upon them. In fact, he always thought he was abnormal for thinking and feeling this way and tried hard not to let anyone know he had such fantasies. It is only in the past couple of years, due to the increasing media coverage of homosexuality, that he has been able to identify himself as gay. He is, however, not comfortable sharing this with anyone and does not want to establish a sexual relationship with a man as he fears the reaction of his family and community.

This means that while a person may primarily be sexually or romantically attracted to persons of his/her own sex, he/she may not establish a romantic or sexual relationship with them due to social or cultural pressures. Such a person's sexual interest or attraction may remain hidden, suppressed or 'in the closet'. In fact, like Narendra, many people of a homosexual orientation, contrary to their innate attraction towards people of their own sex, establish sexual relationships with persons of the opposite sex, marry and have children.

Sexual orientation is not a matter of personal choice but is a biological fact. One's sexual orientation becomes evident as one begins to explore sexuality. It is during the teenage years that young people begin to experience romantic or sexual attraction and this is the time when questions regarding sexual orientation often emerge. The process of exploring and expressing their emerging sexuality and coming to an understanding, acceptance and integration of their sexual identity is a process that all children undergo.

There are many parts to a person's identity. These include gender, ethnic/racial background, socio-cultural background, religion, sexual orientation, and so on. Hence, sexual orientation is just one of many different aspects of a person's identity. Sometimes, the different aspects of one's identity may clash. If that happens, there is great emotional turmoil and one makes an effort to resolve the inner conflict and integrate all aspects of one's identity. An integrated identity implies a feeling of peace within and comfort with oneself, something all human beings strive for.

Homosexuality

The term 'homosexuality', as we use it today across the world, is attributed to the German psychologist Karoly Maria Benkert and was coined in the late nineteenth century. According to a Stanford University paper,[4] which gives a detailed account of the history of homosexuality in the West, the term is relatively new but the sexual activity associated with homosexuality has been discussed and documented in the West from the time of Plato's writings. For example, it has been discussed in Plato's *Symposium*. The ancient Greeks did not divide people into homosexual and heterosexual, but believed that a person could be attracted to either sex. Men could have sexual relationships with other men and be married, or marry a woman later. However, as religious and social realities changed, intolerance towards homosexuality crept in. From the twelfth century onwards, homosexuality became increasingly criminalized, with the death penalty sometimes being imposed.

With time, views about and attitudes towards homosexuality changed again. The Napoleonic Code specifically decriminalized sodomy. Eventually, from viewing homosexual acts as sinful and voluntarily chosen, a more scientific point of view prevailed and homosexuality began to be viewed as biologically driven. From the nineteenth century onwards, therefore, homosexuality was seen more as a medical problem rather than a criminal offence. Attempts were then made to 'treat' homosexuality and 'prevent' children from becoming homosexual.

Gradually, as sex outside of marriage and recreational sex, that is, sex without the purpose of having children, gained more acceptance, homosexuality also became more acceptable. It was in this general context that the gay liberation movement emerged in the 1960s. Eventually, the American Psychiatric Association removed homosexuality from its list of mental disorders in 1973.

Indian authors have confirmed the fact that homosexuality has been documented in India for centuries. Scholars report that religious scriptures, literature and poetry in India have described and explained homosexuality in several ways. They report that several fourteenth-century texts in Sanskrit and Bengali, including *Krittivasa Ramayana*, tell the story of King Bhagiratha who is supposed to have been born from the union between two women.[5, 6] Texts from early Buddhist and Hindu periods, such as *Manusmriti*, *Arthasastra* and *Kama Sutra* also reportedly refer to same-sex attraction and behaviour. The pillar caves of Karle (50–75CE) and several sculptures and carvings in Khajuraho and the Sun Temple of Konarak depict same-sex sexual behaviour.[7]

Bisexuality

The term 'bisexuality' is a derivative of the word 'bisexual'. Bisexuality means being sexually attracted to both men and women. Research has found that while many men and women experience and identify bisexual feelings from childhood onwards, others may initially experience homosexual feelings and later find that they are heterosexually attracted too. At the same time, there are people who become aware of bisexual feelings after being in a heterosexual relationship or marriage.[8]

'Some bi people are more romantically attracted to men and more physically attracted to women. Some bisexuals are attracted to people who conform to mainstream gender norms; some are attracted specifically to people who defy those norms. For some bisexuals, gender is an important part of attraction. For other bi people, it is totally irrelevant if a person is male, female, intersex, or something else. Many bisexuals have very fixed patterns of attraction, while for others, the balance between heterosexual and homosexual attraction is fluid and changes over the years.'[9]

Sexual Identity Development

Elizabeth Morgan's recent review of theories and research in the area of sexual orientation and sexual identity development[10] points out that there is great variation in the journey of individuals. There are young people who are very comfortable with their sexual orientation and have a clear sense of their sexual identity, whether homosexual or heterosexual. They are able to enter adulthood with this comfort and clarity. Then there are young people who begin their explorations regarding their sexual orientation, especially same-sex interests, after they enter adulthood, when they feel more independent from their families. At the same time, young people who have bisexual interests, that is a sexual interest in people of either sex, may feel especially pressurized to adopt one sexual identity, either homosexual or heterosexual.

Sexual identity formation is one of the tasks of adolescence and young adulthood. As sexual identity is one of the multiple identities that young people are sorting through, such as their gender, religious and racial identities, several factors impact and influence sexual identity formation. Larger socio-cultural values, socio-economic status, laws regarding sexual expression, religious values, spirituality, ability, family-specific beliefs and practices, peer group acceptance and personality characteristics—all combine and have an impact on sexual identity development.

Heterosexual identity formation is an easier process to go through. Children are exposed to fairy tales and stories from early childhood onwards that are full of examples of heterosexual relationships. In India, religious texts and socio-cultural practices have established a set of stages that a person is supposed to go through in life where marriage, which is currently defined as the union between a male and a female, is accepted as 'normal' or even ideal. Whether the marriage is arranged by the family or not, it has a socially sanctioned and legally recognized status. While most Indian adults may not display romantic behaviour in public, children are exposed to innumerable examples of heterosexual relationships on a daily basis via television programmes and movies. Developing a heterosexual identity, therefore, does not involve any conscious thought, internal conflict or struggle.

The story is very different when a child does not have a heterosexual orientation. As children grow up and discover that they are sexual beings, they may find that they are naturally attracted to either people of their own sex or the opposite sex or both. This means that they may discover homosexual or bisexual thoughts and feelings. However, due to legal and cultural issues, homosexual identity formation becomes quite a long-drawn-out process. It often extends well into adulthood.

Theories and research in the area of homosexual identity

formation have described how a homosexual/bisexual identity is formed. Some of the theories describe it by talking about phases and others discuss it in terms of processes that occur. Scholars talk about six 'identity processes' that occur during the lesbian or female homosexual, gay or male homosexual, and bisexual (LGB) identity formation.[11] These processes are not dependent on each other, which means that they are not steps that follow one another. Some of them may occur in conjunction with each other and some may last one's entire lifetime. The processes defined are as follows:

Exiting heterosexuality

Exiting implies facing the fact of what one is *not*. Exiting heterosexuality involves facing the fact that one's sexual attraction is not towards a person of the opposite sex. On the part of adolescents, it involves recognizing and accepting the fact that they are not heterosexual, unlike many of their peers, friends or family members. This is one of the most difficult transition phases because it is accompanied with the realization that they are different from others. It may lead to an adolescent thinking that he/she is not 'normal' or is flawed. At a time when young people are trying to fit in with their peers, it can create great anguish for them as being different means that they cannot fit in, will be ridiculed or not accepted.

As sexuality is often not talked about in families, a teenager going through this phase is likely to find it difficult to approach a trusted adult to talk about his/her concerns and fears regarding his/her sexual orientation. Many teenagers may try to hide the fact that they do not see themselves as heterosexual or do not have any heterosexual feelings. In addition to worrying about being accepted by their peers, they may also worry about or fear their parents' reactions to their sexual orientation.

Developing a personal LGB identity

This means accepting and identifying with being lesbian, gay or bisexual. This phase does not involve making a public declaration but is a process that occurs at a personal/private level. It means resolving any internal conflict young people may have, especially if their religious or spiritual identity clashes with their homosexual/bisexual identity. It also implies becoming comfortable with their own view of themselves and with their romantic/sexual interest, and *not* feeling that such thoughts and feelings are wrong or 'abnormal' or need to be changed. It essentially means being able to comfortably say to oneself, 'I am gay/lesbian/bisexual and I am perfectly okay with it.'

Developing an LGB social identity

The LGB social identity develops when young people start sharing their homosexual status with people other than immediate family members. This includes friends, neighbours or work colleagues. This status may also change depending upon the circumstances. For example, some people may be comfortable sharing the fact that they are homosexual with family and friends but may not mention it in a work environment. Or work colleagues at a previous workplace may have known about their homosexuality but they may not be comfortable talking about it at a new workplace. Tim Cook, the Apple CEO, recently established his LGB social identity when he made a very public statement to the media declaring his homosexual status.

Becoming an LGB offspring

For a teenager, this essentially means letting parents know that one does *not* have any heterosexual interests and/or is attracted to people of the same sex or both sexes. While some young people may inform their parents of their homosexuality early on, others may do so only as adults, and some, like Narendra, may never share this information with their family.

Developing an LGB intimacy status

An LGB intimacy status refers to establishing a romantic relationship with a person of the same sex, if one's sexual orientation is homosexual. Alternatively, one could enter into a romantic relationship with a person regardless of their sex, if one's sexual orientation is bisexual. The reality of India, however, is that many people who are gay are not able to openly form intimate relationships, or fear getting into an intimate relationship altogether, due to Section 377 of the Indian Penal Code that criminalizes homosexual behaviour.

Ban Ki-moon, Secretary General of the United Nations, has reportedly taken a strong stand on gay rights and passed several resolutions seeking to end discrimination and violence against the LGBT community worldwide. He has also appealed to the Indian government to change its stance and repeal Section 377 of the Indian Penal code that makes homosexuality a punishable offence.[12] Same-sex marriage, while possible in some parts of the world like Ireland and the Netherlands, is not yet possible in India. Until India changes its regressive legal stance on homosexual behaviour and same-sex marriages, developing an LGB intimacy status will continue to be full of risks.

Entering an LGB community

If an LGB community exists, then a person with a homosexual or bisexual orientation can join such a community and find support through this association. However, in India, LGB communities as organized entities are few. Hence, the option of socializing with others who share the same sexual orientation is somewhat within reach in big cities but virtually impossible in smaller towns.

Individuals vary in their progress while going through these processes. For example, a person may have a strong LGB social identity and an intimate same-sex partner, but not have come out as an LGB to their family (*not* become an LGB offspring). Further, depending on the context and timing, they may go back and forth in a given process, such as when openly LGB people enter a new work setting, they may choose not to express their LGB identity.

In fact, given all the socio-cultural and legal issues, there are some people who may not even go through all the processes ever in their lives. Therefore, in accordance with this model of sexual identity formation, some Indians may never be able to fully form or integrate their sexual identity because homosexuality does not have a legally or socially sanctioned status in India. In other words, there are many children who may never be able to fully attain a cohesive and integrated identity, that is, they will struggle internally and externally to be accepted for something that is innate to them and cannot be changed.

As parents, we need to work towards changing the laws of our country and increase our awareness, understanding and sensitivity, especially with regard to homosexuality and bisexuality. Unless we do so, we will unnecessarily penalize and cause anguish to those children who are not heterosexual.

Transgender, Gender Diverse, Genderqueer and Cross-dressing Children and Youth

All children at some point in their growing up years discover two important things—gender and sexuality. In fact, gender is a construct that children everywhere discover quite early in life as it exists in all societies. Children may feel comfortable and identify with the gender that is socially ascribed to them or they may feel discomfort in the gender they are born with.

This process is different from a young person disagreeing with roles or behaviour assigned to different genders. For example, there are girls who may not agree with their community or family's ideas regarding personal behaviour, education and career choices. However, they may be very comfortable identifying themselves as female.

Gender identity comes into question, for example, when a male child thinks and feels that he is actually a female child, or vice versa. The discomfort felt by such children is not with gender roles and expectations. Their discomfort is very fundamentally with the gender that they are supposed to be, based on the sex they were born with. It is in effect a conflict with one's biology. This experience is conveyed in the words of Ludovic Fabre, the 'girlboy' in the movie *Ma Vie en Rose*, 'To make a baby, parents play tic-tac-toe. When one wins, God sends Xs and Ys. XX for a girl, and XY for a boy. But my X for a girl fell in the trash, and I got a Y instead. See? A scientific error! But God will fix it and send me an X and make me a girl and then we'll get married, okay?'

Transgender and Gender Diverse

In India, the term transgender often brings to mind images of Hijras (eunuchs) dancing at weddings or standing at traffic lights, demanding money from people in return for blessings. While Hijras as a community are accepted as a part of Indian society and are ascribed a role at Hindu weddings or births, they are not integrated into society as such, and find it difficult to live, study or work in varied professions. The Hijras have a lifestyle of their own and live in segregated communities. Most people join the Hijra community for different reasons, mainly socio-economic ones. Indian scholars have traced the history of individuals who cross-dress or are transgendered to epics such as the Mahabharata and Ramayana.[13]

Hijras may be technically described as transgender as they are men who have adopted a female gender identity and, in some cases, have undergone castration. But all transgender individuals in India are not part of the Hijra community. In fact, most transgender folks across the world do not live in separate communities. They live and work alongside those who are not transgender.

A person is referred to as transgender when his/her self-identity does not conform unambiguously to conventional notions of male or female gender. This discomfort essentially with the sex (male or female) that one is born with often emerges in childhood. It gets stronger as the child grows and social expectations to conform to gender-defined behaviour increase.

'Transgender is an umbrella term for persons whose gender identity, gender expression or behaviour does not conform to that typically associated with the sex to which they were assigned at birth. Gender identity refers to a person's internal sense of being male, female or something else; gender expression refers to the way a person communicates gender identity to others through behaviour, clothing, hairstyles, voice or body characteristics.'[14]

Gender identity and sexual orientation are two separate concepts. Gender identity refers to one's own sense of being a man or woman and sexual orientation refers to the gender one feels sexually or romantically attracted to. Children begin to have a sense of their gender identity between the ages of two and five years. Hence, children who are transgender or gender diverse may begin to play in a way that is very different from other children of their sex from an early age. Some children who are transgender will grow up to have heterosexual relationships, others may be bisexual or homosexual relative to the gender they identify with.[15, 16]

'Gender diverse' (also known as gender nonconforming, gender creative, or gender variant) is a term used for children and youth who prefer clothes, accessories, hair-length/styles, or activities that differ from what is socio-culturally expected for their sex. Some of these children may feel comfortable with their biological sex but look or act like the opposite gender. Some of them may be uncomfortable with their biological sex or gender but not to the extent that they want to change their gender. There may be others, though, who may explore options for transitioning to the opposite gender.

Socially, boys who are gender diverse face stronger negative reactions from their parents and peers than gender-diverse girls. 'This is due to the great latitude given to girls expressing masculine behaviours in a society that overvalues male behaviours and undervalues female behaviours.'[17, 18]

Transgender children and youth, on the other hand, 'typically consistently, persistently, and insistently express a cross-gender identity and feel that their gender is different from their assigned sex.'[19, 20] Such children and adolescents feel very uncomfortable with the fact that their biological sex does not match with their sense of their gender.

While some transgender children are able to express that they are of the opposite gender from the time they begin to talk, others do so around puberty or later. Some also feel a deep sense of discomfort with their bodies due to this mismatch. Such teenagers may wish to socially, legally or medically change their gender while they are still in school.

Why some children are transgender is not clear, but what is

clear is that children and teenagers do not become transgender because of their family environment. Aadya, also known as Gopala, is a six-year-old transgender child. During his infancy and early childhood, his mother would dress him up in frocks with clips and hairbands because of his biological female sex. Around the age of three, however, Aadya/Gopala on his own began insisting on keeping his hair short and wearing boys' clothes. Aadya/Gopala would refer to himself as 'Gopala' and insist that he was a boy. When talking in Hindi, he would refer to himself using the male pronoun.

While using the opposite gender pronoun is fairly common among young children, if corrected, they change it, and most children self-correct gender usage by the age of seven. Children who are transgender, like Aadya/Gopala, however, resist changing it as they feel that they are already using the correct pronoun. In Aadya/Gopala's case, his gender nonconforming behaviour does not go down well with his peers and teachers. As a result, he has a difficult time at school. Feeling unhappy and isolated, he sometimes withdraws and, at other times, gets into fights with his peers. Luckily for him, though, both his parents are very supportive of him and accept his transgender identity as a male.

While there is a small possibility that Aadya/Gopala may change his ideas about his gender as he grows, it is most likely that based on his strong belief that he is a boy, he will continue to see and experience himself as one. By adolescence, gender identity becomes 'very resistant, if not immutable, to any type of environmental intervention.'[21, 22] Hence, if Aadya's gender identity continues to be that of a male, by the time he reaches his teenage years, it is not likely to change at all. Moreover, any efforts—however gentle, now or later—to get him to change his gender identity are likely to add to the sense of isolation and unhappiness felt by this young child.

The Different Expressions of Gender and Sexuality

Recently, on the popular TV show *Satyameva Jayate*, Aamir Khan (actor and anchor) interviewed a young lady, Ghazal, who was born as a male into a north Indian family. She went through childhood and adolescence as a boy who did not feel comfortable being a boy. Ultimately, as an adult, she informed her parents about her unhappiness at being a man and her deeply felt desire to be the woman she thought and felt she was. Ghazal's family was extremely supportive and helped her transition from being born a male to becoming a female.

Such cases, where a person has been able to transition to the opposite gender with the complete support of their family, are still few. But parental support is very important as it helps individuals like Ghazal feel happy, confident and comfortable with themselves.

Cross-dressers

'People who cross-dress wear clothing that is traditionally or stereotypically worn by another gender in their culture. They vary in how completely they cross-dress, from one article of clothing to fully cross-dressing. Those who cross-dress are usually comfortable with their assigned sex and do not wish to change it. Cross-dressing is a form of gender expression and is not necessarily tied to erotic activity. Cross-dressing is not indicative of sexual orientation.'[23] 'Drag Kings', women who dress up as men, and 'Drag Queens', men who dress up as women, are cross-dressers who usually dress up and perform at clubs and other such places.

For cross-dressing children and teenagers 'lack of acceptance by family and friends can result in many problems. Loneliness and isolation is a common theme for young people and, especially, if they feel different from everyone else. A young boy wishing to dress up like a girl, sneaking away with clothes from his mother or his sister and then trying them on privately, will often feel a great burden from having to keep his activity such a huge secret'.[24] Young people who cross-dress may fear being discovered and feel guilty as they may think what they are doing is wrong. They may also feel confused, especially when sexual feelings arise. Cross-dressing teenagers may be homosexual or heterosexual. Many cross-dressers may go on to marry and have children.[25]

Genderqueer

'Genderqueer is a term that some people use who identify their gender as falling outside the binary constructs of "male" and "female". They may define their gender as falling somewhere on a continuum between male and female, or they may define it as wholly different from these terms.'[26]

Steps parents can take to support their child

Educate yourself

Look at your own biases, prejudices or religious beliefs that may come in the way of being supportive of children and young people who have a different sexual orientation or gender identity from your own. A lot of one's inherent discomfort is really learnt discomfort based on the influences of one's family and the larger society.

Seek out opportunities to educate yourself about these issues. For example, *Ma Vie en Rose* is a lovely French film released in 1997 whose main character is a seven-year-old transgender girl, Ludovic Fabre. The movie very sensitively captures the experiences of a young transgender child and the challenges she faces because her gender identity is different from that of others.

There are many Indian organizations that work on LGBT

issues, such as Sahodari Foundation, NAZ Foundation, ABVA, the Humsafar Trust, Sangama (which carries a list of self-help groups, communities and organizations across different cities), that can be accessed for information and support.

In recognition of the fact that people who are transgender, especially Hijras, often face enormous difficulties due to discrimination and abuse, the Supreme Court has granted the right to not self-identify as male or female. 'The court also directed the central and state governments to take the necessary steps to allow for equal status by ensuring adequate healthcare, education and employment as well as separate public toilets and numerous other safeguards against discrimination. All identity documents such as birth certificates, passports and driver's licences will now have a third gender box.[27] It is now up to us as parents to make sure that these steps are implemented.

Help your child develop and integrate his/her sexual identity

As mentioned earlier, Aamir Khan, on his show *Satyameva Jayate*, interviewed a confident young man who appeared to be very comfortable with his sexuality and talked about his parents being a big source of support for him. When this young man disclosed to his parents that he did not feel attracted to women and was interested in men instead, his parents admitted that they were unable to understand his experience. At the same time, they accepted his experience as valid and did not ask him to change himself in any way. The fact that they did not get upset, criticize him, express anger, disappointment or any other such strong negative emotions, helped him feel good about himself.

Recently, a matrimonial advertisement was placed in a Mumbai-based tabloid by Padma Iyer, mother of gay rights activist Harish Iyer, for her gay son. Reportedly, Padma's initial attempts to get the same ad published failed as three major newspapers rejected her application, citing legal or other issues.[28] While this is an example of how India, at a societal level, continues to be conservative and close-minded, it is also an example of how individuals and families are able to assert their right to happiness and personal freedom. Most importantly, it demonstrates how family support plays an immense role in helping individuals, no matter what their sexual orientation or gender identity is, be comfortable with themselves and live happy and fulfilled lives.

'Lesbian, gay and bisexual youth who do well despite stress—like all adolescents who do well despite stress—tend to be those who are socially competent, who have good problem-solving skills, who have a sense of autonomy and purpose, and who look forward to the future.'[29] These are all qualities that parents can encourage in all children. More specifically, the current advice from mental health professionals from across the world, including Indian psychiatrists, is that adolescents and young people who are exploring and expressing their homosexuality should not be seen as psychiatrically ill and should be supported in their effort to express their sexuality.[30]

In India, children have very little or no exposure to people in the family, school, community or even the media who are openly homosexual and are accepted for it. Many teenagers may not even have a name for their experience—they may or may not have heard of the terms 'gay', 'lesbian' or 'bisexual'. They may not know that their sexual feelings are normal and there are other adolescents who think and feel like them. This situation can push a teenager towards isolation and increase his/her vulnerability to mental health issues, such as depression and suicide.[31]

Hence, this early phase of discovery, when the child may be in his mid to late teens and early adulthood, is the most crucial phase when parental understanding and support means a lot for the healthy development of the child. Some teenagers may attempt to let their parents know about their homosexuality during the teenage years, but if they feel their parents are not receptive to the idea, they may not take the conversation further.

It is very important for parents to be aware and educate themselves on sexual orientation issues. In addition, it is important to create an environment of acceptance at home for all variations of human experience by showing acceptance and respect for people who may be gay/lesbian or are openly gay/lesbian. Jokes and mockery of known or unknown people who are gay, lesbian or bisexual indirectly communicates a lack of acceptance. Desist from engaging in such behaviour yourself and intervene if and when you see children and teenagers showing intolerance—teach them to respect all human beings.

Help your child express his/her gender identity

Research suggests that for children who are transgender or show gender-diverse behaviours, family support and a sense of a positive future are factors that help develop a healthy social and emotional life. Family support in this context would mean, first of all, accepting whatever the child believes his/her gender to be, and then helping the child become more comfortable with himself/herself, without trying to change or eliminate cross-gender behaviour. 'Children who experience affirming and supportive responses to their gender identity are more likely to have improved mental health outcomes. Gender identity is resistant if not impervious to environmental manipulation. Moreover, attempts to change a child's gender may have a negative impact on the child's well-being.'[32] Therefore, do not try to talk, coax, coerce or threaten the child into changing his/her gender nonconforming behaviour.

This means that as a parent, one needs to become comfortable with any ambiguity that exists in a young child's gender expression. While accepting a child's gender nonconforming behaviour is the first and most important step, as a supportive parent, you can do more. Help the child explore and express his/her experience of gender, and talk to him/her about gender in a developmentally appropriate manner. It is also important to explain your child's experience to other family members and friends and get them to be supportive of your child's gender expression. In addition, advocate for your child in his/her school and community settings, when required, so that he/she does not have to face discrimination and harassment.[33] As a parent or concerned adult, you can also 'advocate for gender diverse and transgender students in schools by providing education, recommending that schools create and implement policies and procedures to prevent harassment, honour students' preferred names and pronouns, ensure bathroom safety for all students, allow access to all possible gender-segregated activities that honour all students' gender identities'.[34]

Sometimes, teenagers and young adults express the desire to physically change their appearance to match the gender that they experience as theirs. 'Early medical intervention is recommended for peri-pubertal transgender youth who have a history of gender dysphoria and a desire to live as another gender. Puberty delaying treatment, cross sex hormone treatment, and/or surgical intervention(s) may be indicated to treat gender dysphoria.'[35] While puberty-delaying treatment is indicated for children who are unsure and need some time to make up their minds fully about their gender, the other interventions are irreversible sex-change interventions. If you think these interventions will benefit your child or your child wants to consider these, you should consult medical and mental health professionals who have an understanding of transgender issues.

Chapter 4

PITFALLS AND PERILS OF THE INTERNET

The challenge is that children are the "digital natives", and parents are the "digital immigrants". Children are "native speakers" of the digital language of computers, video games, and the Internet, and many parents have not been able to develop digital proficiency. Parents are often left feeling overwhelmed, uninformed, or ill-equipped to adequately protect their kids online.
—Enough is Enough (EIE)

The Internet is a gold mine of information. At the same time, the information available is indiscriminate and unedited—there is no 'Adult' grading for the information, photos and videos that turn up on searches the moment a device is turned on. While children can access the Internet from the safety and security of their home, they become unsafe the moment the Internet is accessed. All the risks that exist in the real world exist in the virtual one. Children can be exposed to information they are not mature enough to understand or process, such as pornography, bullying and sexual abuse.

Pornography of all kinds, including what has been described as 'hardcore porn' or 'rape porn', is freely available on the Internet. Exposure to pornography, especially such extreme forms, can be very confusing, disturbing and upsetting for young people. Children are also vulnerable to harassment and bullying from peers as well as exposed to sexual predators and stalkers. Just like poor decisions, such as early sexual activity or alcohol and drug use, can have a very negative impact on children, decisions online, such as sharing personal information and photographs or making virtual friends they know nothing about, can also pose dangers.

The Internet never switches off. Most teenagers, anyway, tend to stay up late at night due to changes in the brain's regulation of the sleep–wake cycle. The Internet accentuates that tendency. However, adequate sleep is necessary for optimal brain functioning, since lack of sleep leads to fatigue, difficulty maintaining attention, irritability and depression. Studies with adolescents show that sleep deprivation is also involved in increased impulsive behaviour and possibly delinquent behaviour.[1]

Impulsive behaviour that teenagers sometimes engage in include early sexual activity, experimenting with smoking, alcohol and drugs. As the adolescent brain is still developing and does not stop doing so until a person reaches his/her twenties, intoxicating substances have a greater effect. For example, when adolescents drink alcohol, they seem to imbibe larger quantities than adults. Drinking in youth and drinking large quantities are both connected to alcohol dependence in adulthood. Research has also shown that even small quantities of nicotine are enough to get the adolescent brain addicted, while adults require more. Although the addictive influence of the Internet is still being studied, it is highly likely that the still developing adolescent brain is similarly more at risk from any such addiction than researchers establish.

Pornography exposure and its impact

Young people have always been curious about sex. However, a couple of decades ago, the only way children came close to accessing sexually explicit material was through novels describing sex or through movies. Such content usually left a lot to the imagination. Some older teens may have viewed adult magazines, such as *Playboy*, or even watched adult films, but access to these was never easy.

With all kinds of content finding its way to the Internet, all behaviours imaginable are available, unedited, to children of all ages. Children as young as two years old who can easily operate an iPad can as easily find adult pornographic content. There are no barriers to access, and it is all freely available. In fact, children as young as fourteen and fifteen are confidently being able to navigate around the Internet and seek out pornography.

Hence, there is 'either intentionally or accidentally, sexually explicit material online, from adult pornography (the kind of images that appear in *Playboy*) to prosecutable material depicting graphic sex acts, live sex shows, orgies, bestiality, and violence. Even material depicting the actual sexual abuse of a child (child pornography)—once only found on the black market—is instantly available and accessible on the Internet. Through the Internet, much of this aberrant material has entered the mainstream, directly impacting our children's healthy sexual development'.[2]

It is alarming how children stumble upon pornography in multiple ways on the Internet. Even those who do not seek it out are bombarded with pornographic images. Studies have found that adolescents commonly stumble upon sexually explicit material while searching for absolutely unrelated information. In one study, 42 per cent of adolescents reported exposure to pornography online, with 66 per cent of those teens describing such exposure as unsought, unwanted. The pornography industry also does not deny access to children who are underage; 66 per cent of pornography websites studied did not display any adult content warning. In fact, 75 per cent of pornographic websites were found to display visual teasers on the homepage before enquiring about a person's age, and only 3 per cent required a viewer's proof of age. Also, smartphones, which are becoming ubiquitous, do not have filtering systems for Internet access.[3, 4]

Pornography websites often use innocuous means to reach out to people. The indirect ways in which such websites catch children's attention is through innocent word searches, misspelled words, using 'stealth sites' with web addresses that are similar to more regularly used websites, pop-ups, cartoon characters and child icons, free flash games, and spam or junk emails.[5]

It is through such means that Samar, a fifteen-year-old boy from a well-to-do, well-educated family who studies at a reputed school in Gurgaon, got caught in the pornography trap. Unable to share his feelings with anyone else, he confided in his counsellor that he was quite disturbed after viewing 'rape porn'. He found himself experiencing a mixture of fascination and revulsion on watching the images. Moreover, the images would stay in his mind long afterwards and would continue to disturb and distract him.

A year later, following a series of discussions about these images, Samar was able to move past his morbid fascination for such pornography. He is also fortunate to have parents who discussed the impact of media and gender issues with him so that he was able to form a more sensitive approach towards others, specifically in the context of intimate relationships. However, other children are not as fortunate. Samar often talked about his friends who also viewed such pornographic content on the net, but remained entangled in its web. They even showed a change in behaviour, such as tending to act violently towards their girlfriends.

It is a matter of concern how behaviour such as watching

pornography can easily become 'normal' because most of a teenager's peers do it. While watching pornography at this age a generation ago would have been considered an aberration, for the current generation it is becoming 'normal'. While watching pornography may become a usual part of Internet viewing, its impact is still very negative as children do not have the cognitive or emotional maturity to process such information.

Research has confirmed that long-term, frequent exposure to pornography can create misperceptions amongst adolescents about sexual activity, including unrealistic expectations regarding sex, sexual preoccupations, perpetuating permissible attitudes, sexual callousness and a negative attitude towards one's sexual partner.[6] In addition, such exposure also leads to less progressive gender role attitudes, greater sexual activity as well as a tendency in males to perpetrate sexual harassment.[7]

Quite alarmingly, adolescents have also been found to 'normalize' being sexually abused due to exposure to pornography. In general, female adolescents exposed to pornography feel physically inferior and are at a greater risk of becoming victims of sexual violence as well as contracting sexually transmitted diseases.[8] At the same time, what is worrying is the lack of awareness among parents about their child's access to pornography. A study of sexually abusive children showed that 25 per cent of these children had accessed pornography through an older sibling or peer. This is while the parents were completely unaware of this and were under the delusion that their child would never watch pornography on the Internet.[9]

Online sexual predators

Neha is a fourteen-year-old girl whose best friend, Ahana, relocated to the US a few years ago. When Ahana visited Neha over the summer vacations, she told Neha about her friends who lived in Bangalore. Then, one day, she asked Neha to accompany her to the nearby mall as both her friends from Bangalore were going to come down to meet her. At that point, she admitted to Neha that she had never met either of the boys before, and that they were her virtual friends. Neha shared this information with her mother, who got alarmed and decided to accompany the girls. It turned out that the two were, indeed, older boys but not adults. The girls were lucky.

There have been cases of adults pretending to be teenagers online and, often, these adults can be sexual predators. *To Catch a Predator* ran as a very popular American reality television series on the newsmagazine *Dateline NBC*. It showed scores of potential 'child predators' being caught. Each of these adults had befriended a young person, who they knew was a minor, on an Internet chat room. Some of them had indulged in sexual conversations with the minor, then took the young person's address and turned up to meet them. Since this was a reality show, the situations were all 'set-ups' and the young people were actually volunteers of an NGO working towards exposing online predation.[10] Hence, no harm occurred on the show—the potential child predators were trapped and, in some cases, arrested.

Sexting and Revenge Porn

Connect Safely, a US-based organization, defines sexting as 'the sharing of nude or semi-nude and sexually provocative photos via cellphone but it can happen on other devices and the Web too. First of all, research shows most teens don't "sext" and most of those who do experience no negative consequences. But for teens who do sext, there are both psychological and legal risks, especially if coercion is involved and the images wind up being distributed beyond their intended audience'.[11]

Pitfalls and Perils of the Internet

The unintended distribution of such images, which might have been taken intentionally or unintentionally or through the use of coercion, is also called revenge porn. Such an act often occurs after the break-up of a romantic/intimate relationship or may involve an abusive relationship.[12]

Scholars, who have looked at a wide variety of studies on this topic, point out that it is not yet possible to accurately estimate the number of teenagers sexting, but they assure us that only a small number of teenagers do so. One of the American studies found that 4 per cent of the twelve to seventeen-year-olds interviewed had sent a nude or nearly nude photo or video of themselves to someone; the older teens were more likely to have done so than the younger ones. This research found no difference in the number of boys and girls who had sent such sexts.[13]

Whatever may be the exact numbers, there is a real danger of teenagers sharing such images via the web with people they do not know, or with adults who may be pressurizing them to share their photographs. While teenagers may share such images or texts with other teenagers with whom they are in a consensual relationship, and it may not result in any negative consequences,[14] often such sharing can become highly problematic.

Occasionally, there are reports of nude or semi-nude photographs of film stars or other prominent persons being leaked and published on the Internet or newspapers/magazines. The same situation can befall unsuspecting teenagers too. In 2004, as two students from a prominent New Delhi school were having sex on the campus, the boy took a video of the act on his cellphone. Later, this video became public and both the students involved were reportedly expelled from the school. The young boy had a warrant issued against him for making such a video, and an IIT student was arrested for circulating the

MMS and selling it to Bazee.com. The Bazee.com CEO was arrested for displaying the video on its website for three days and making and selling CDs of the video clip.[15, 16]

If a sex video intentionally or unintentionally becomes public, it does have a social and psychological impact on the lives of the children/young people involved. It may leave them feeling socially ostracized, embarrassed or ashamed. In addition, actions taken against them, such as expulsion from school or legal proceedings, can further negatively impact a child's life.

The Pew Research Center's study on 'Teens and Sexting'[17] has identified some factors that seem to increase or decrease the chances of a teenager sending a sext. They found that 75 per cent of the teenagers who had unlimited text messaging plans had received suggestive texts, and 18 per cent had received nude or nearly nude photos and videos. Some teenagers protected access to sexual images with passwords so that their parents could not come across these pictures or messages.

While some teenagers who were part of the study viewed sexting as normal teenage behaviour, others did not. Some of the older teenagers interviewed stated that often girls sext because they feel pressured into doing so by the boy they are interested in. In some cases, sexting occurred because the girl felt the boy would leave the relationship or not be interested in her if she did not send it. Some teens, however, saw it as a safer alternative to actually having sex. Teens who sent sexts also seemed to be among those who spend a large amount of time on their cellphones and use them as a major source of entertainment.

On the other hand, the study found that teenagers whose parents paid for their cellphones, and had a limited messaging plan, were less likely to send sexts. Only 8 per cent of those on a limited plan and 4 per cent of those who paid per message had received sexts. For some teenagers, the fact that their parents would often check their cellphones acted as a deterrent. Others stated they did not sext because they were scared of school policies or the legal ramifications of sexting. Some also worried about the social impact of the sexts becoming public.

Cyberbullying

A 2012 research, commissioned by Microsoft Corporation, indicated that 53 per cent of the children surveyed in India, between the ages of eight and seventeen, who use the Internet, reported being cyberbullied, that is, threatened or harassed online.[18] A more recent 2014 McAffee study (McAfee is a part of Intel Security, the security software company) with teenagers in the US has reported that 87 per cent of those who participated in the study had witnessed cyberbullying. While 72 per cent of those who were bullied stated that it was related to their appearance, 26 per cent said it was due to race or religion, and 22 per cent stated their sexuality was the reason for the bullying.

The reason why cyberbullying is worrying is because it has a real psychological impact on the person being bullied. The McAfee study found that 53 per cent of the teenagers who had witnessed bullying reported that the victims became defensive or angry, while 47 per cent said the victims deleted their social media accounts. In addition, online behaviour affects offline behaviour—50 per cent of the teenagers surveyed in the same study said they got into an argument due to comments being posted on social media, and 4 per cent had got into an actual physical fight because of an online argument.

Creating a 'Digital Fortress' for Safe Navigation of the Internet

Based on real incidents of online sexual predators targeting children and teenagers, the FBI has come up with guidelines for parents to prevent children from being exploited online.[19] End to Cyber Bullying, a US based non-profit, also recommends several steps to protect children and prevent cyberbullying.[20] Research also indicates what may help. The following are some suggestions for ensuring the safety of children who use digital media based on all the following recommendations:

Inform

Information is power. Talk to children across age groups about the dangers of the Internet. It is important to do so as children and teenagers may access the Internet on their friend's phone or on a computer elsewhere. Hence, they need to be empowered so that they can make sound decisions, especially when accessing digital media unsupervised.

Explain to children that all kinds of people use the Internet for all kinds of reasons. In an age-appropriate manner, tell them that they need to watch out for bullies as well as people who may sometimes try to fool them or harm them in some way. Let young children know that the Internet contains a plethora of information, some of which is inappropriate for them. Teenagers often surf the web independently and it is important to help them identify credible websites from where they can access information independently. All that appears on the Internet is not true and they should verify the information they come across in websites.

Children also need to know what your expectations are in terms of Internet/phone usage and behaviour related to these devices. Let children know that once a picture is posted or something is written online, it cannot be taken back. It also has the potential of being accessed by people other than their friends and misused. Hence, it is important to think carefully before posting messages or photographs.

Considering the fact that most Indian teenagers now have cellphones and most of these are smartphones equipped with very high-quality cameras, it becomes imperative that one talks to teenagers about sexting and its dangers. It is important to discuss with teenagers the legal, social and psychological ramifications of sending or receiving sexts, especially photographs. With adolescents it is also important to discuss sexual victimization and the ploys used by online predators.

Monitor

Be aware of the websites and activities your child engages in on the Internet. Just as you would not leave a child unaccompanied in a mall or busy marketplace in the real world, do not leave your child alone with unmonitored access to the virtual world. Keep the computer in a common room and do not allow children access to the Internet in their bedrooms.

Do not allow children to have Internet access on their smartphones as phone Internet usage is more difficult to monitor. Monitoring the child's phone, limiting the usage plan, regulating usage in terms of time spent on the phone, photograph sharing, times during the day when phone usage is allowed, and so on, may help keep your child stay safe.

It is important to very closely monitor your child's use of online chat rooms. Help him/her set up the highest privacy settings for their profiles on sites, such as Facebook or other sites, which ask for factual, identifying, or contact information.

Last, but not the least, set up passwords for your child's web-based accounts and ensure that you know the passwords for phones, computers and web-based accounts. Explain to children your need to know these passwords and let them know you would occasionally be viewing their accounts.

As much as 45 per cent of the children surveyed in the US

about their online activities stated that they would change their behaviour if they knew their parents might be watching their online activities.[21] So, just knowing that parents may be watching is a deterrent and encourages safer and better online behaviour.

Instal parental controls

Find out about any parental controls that your Internet service-provider may offer. Use parental controls provided by various software companies and websites, including Microsoft, YouTube and Apple, among others. Research the latest filtering or blocking softwares available and download them for all the devices accessed by your children, including smartphones. Malware, spyware and viruses are always getting updated and new ones are constantly released. Hence, it is important to keep abreast of the latest, updated versions of anti-virus, blocking and filtering software and download them for all the devices used in the home.

Set up rules

It is important to set up clear and specific rules for Internet behaviour. Tell your children that they should inform you when they make any virtual friends, that is, online friends whom they have never met. In addition, if a virtual friend ever wants to meet them, they must tell you about this. Explain to them that they can meet their virtual friends but you would need to meet those 'friends' first.

Tell children they should avoid uploading any photographs of themselves onto the Internet or online service and to never share photographs of themselves with strangers or virtual friends. Children should also never share their contact information, including name, home address, phone numbers or school name on the Internet. They should check with you before downloading images or information from unknown sources.

Just as you would intervene with offline behaviour, do so with online behaviour. Help children understand from a young age that the words they use online or via messaging have the same impact as they do offline. As you would ask children to report bullying behaviour or stand up for anyone they think is being bullied, do the same for any such behaviour that they observe online. Tell children that they should never respond to messages or bulletin board postings that are suggestive, obscene, belligerent or harassing.

At the same time, keep communication open with teenagers about romantic relationships, the importance of self-respect and mutual respect in relationships, resisting peer pressure and not doing anything they feel uncomfortable about, specifically involving the use of technology—phones and the Internet. The effort and time you invest in taking specific steps and communicating with your children about safety when using digital media will go a long way in helping them make healthy decisions now and in the future.

Chapter 5

IMPACT OF A HIGHLY SEXUALIZED WORLD: HYPER-SEXUALITY AND BODY IMAGE CONCERNS

If you listen to the likes of Yo Yo
You're gonna feel like shit so go slow
You're iridescent, magnificent, triumphant
You'll see the light.
Condescending and they're descending.
You're ascending up the wall
No pumpkin carriage, arranged marriage
Not just melt off the ball
No pear-shaped body and a heart-shaped face
I'm in the open with a pocket full of mace
Survive, defy, resist
You are deferred, not undeterred
Baby it's not Maybelline, it's you
You're not just a masterpiece, you're the painter too.
—'Open Letter to Yo Yo Honey Singh' by
Rene Sharanya Verma

Children and youth in today's age are exposed to a phenomenal variety of media. We have seen a sea-change in the types, availability, access and content of media available. A Price Waterhouse Cooper report for the year 2006 stated that the Indian entertainment and media (E&M) industry was one of the fastest growing sectors in India and was estimated at INR 353 billion in the same year. Television formed 42 per cent, print media 31 per cent and films 19 per cent of the value.[1] This obviously implies that stakes are high and major media efforts are on to reach as many people of different age groups as possible, to influence what they watch, how they behave, what they consume.

While growing up in the 1970s in India, young people largely had access only to movies and audio music. The 1980s added television, and the 1990s brought the Internet. However, by and large, access to the media was still regulated and limited. Children could watch movies only if their parents took them to the movie hall or bought film videos. Many homes did not have a television and those that did, normally had only one, which was shared by all family members and occasionally with neighbours.

The music one listened to was largely that played by the local radio station and the channels were very limited. To a large extent, music was also a shared experience as usually there was only one radio or music system in the house. With the advent of the Walkman, audio music became a more personalized experience. Even then, the music cassettes that could be bought depended upon parental approval, as they were the ones paying, and the choice of music available was also limited to what the stores stocked.

Now, none of the old barriers to information and exposure exist. Children can listen to music on phones and computers via Internet access. Some children have their own computers or have access to the Internet via smartphones. The Internet allows uncensored access to music, films and videos that can be viewed or downloaded with little or no difficulty. Most children, therefore, have unhindered access to music and videos of all kinds.

Parental intervention or influence, as far as music is

concerned, is often minimal or non-existent. While we all expect sexuality to be a major part of movies, a US study on media consumed by seventh and eighth graders found that the music they hear actually contained the most sexual content (40 per cent), followed by movies (12 per cent), and then television (11 per cent).[2]

How does indiscriminate media exposure affect children?

Indian research on the impact of media on children and adolescents is scarce.[3] However, the fact that Indian children and youth, especially those in big cities, have exposure and access to all the media influences of the West makes studies from the West relevant and applicable. In addition, Indian films, especially in terms of definitions of physical attractiveness and social mores, such as premarital sex, are increasingly incorporating Western definitions. The obsession with 'size zero' bodies for female actors and hyper-muscularity for male actors has been completely embraced. Even a 'family' film like *PK* alludes to premarital sex between the lead actress and her boyfriend, which is not considered a major departure from the norm, at least in the movies!

Music, movies, television and magazines, all have an impact on the developing sexuality of adolescents. Some teenagers exposed to the overwhelming sexual content from these sources seem to get involved in sexual activity, including sexual intercourse, much earlier than they otherwise would have.[4, 5] Other teenagers, however, are more influenced by their family's expectations and friends' sexual behaviour.[6] It is important to remember, though, that the media does not influence just one person—it has an impact on an entire generation as everyone is exposed to the same media. Hence, a child who is more influenced by his/her friends than the media is indirectly affected by it. Media influence is, therefore, difficult to escape.

A child's developmental level also influences her readiness to be influenced by the media and, in turn, the decision to engage in sexual activity. Research has reported that girls, regardless of age or race, who enter puberty earlier tend to be more interested in seeing sexual scenes and pictures in movies, television and magazines, and in listening to sexual content in music. In addition, they tend to interpret the sexuality related messages from the media as approving of teens having sexual intercourse.[7]

'There is a major disconnect between what mainstream media portrays—casual sex and sexuality with no consequences—and what children and teenagers need—straightforward information about human sexuality and the need for contraception when having sex. Television, film, music, and the Internet are all becoming increasingly sexually explicit, yet information on abstinence, sexual responsibility and birth control remains rare.'[8]

Magazines and books

Magazines have existed for decades and have been sources of inspiration and aspiration for young people. They have always been referenced for fashion tips regarding the latest hair and clothing styles, colour combinations, and so on. Magazines have also been a source of aspiration for young people who want to look like the people featured in magazines, most of whom are very slim or underweight female models and very muscular male models. The models seem happy and successful, both socially and financially, and it appears that being attractive is the key to such achievement. 'Attractive', according to these magazines, implies being very slim or very muscular and there are few exceptions.

The very restrictive definition of 'attractive' is further reinforced by how the media portrays film stars. Indian female actors, who until a few decades ago tended to be a more healthy weight and more representative of the average young woman, are size zero or thereabouts. Actresses Karishma Kapoor and Sonakshi Sinha's weight loss and figure maintenance programmes are discussed in a positive light, while Aishwarya Rai and Vidya Balan's weight gain are seen in a negative light. A recent *Times of India Online* article titled 'Actresses and their problem areas' criticized some popular female actresses for their weight gain. Despite acknowledging that they have different genetic body shapes/types, it held them responsible for not adhering to an ideal figure with no accumulation of fat.

Articles such as these not only put pressure on the actresses but also convey the message that a person who does not achieve such an ideal shape is lazy or deficient in some way. These articles give no consideration to health, in the sense that exercise and diet are seen as the means to attain this strictly defined ideal shape/size instead of a way to stay healthy. In addition, most magazines emphasize heterosexual relationships as being central to the lives of girls and women, and push the idea that certain cosmetics or clothing will lead them to achieve a specific definition of beauty or attractiveness.[9]

Young men are also under pressure. Gone are the days when the male film lead could be overweight. Male actors have to display a well-toned body, ideally a 'six pack'. The ideal for the male hero is a hyper-muscular physique. Again, hyper-muscular does not necessarily mean a healthy body. In fact, the supplements and steroids used to develop such a physique have a detrimental effect on health.

These messages, unfortunately, not only affect teenagers and young women. Alarmingly, younger and younger children are absorbing these ridiculous notions. Research indicates that one's body image is usually formed around the age of twelve–thirteen years,[10] but children today show a desire for thinness and fear of obesity at younger ages.[11] Recently, a father overheard his five-year-old daughter discuss with her friend how being thin was 'good'. Hence, children as young as five years are becoming concerned about their body image.

Scholars and parents have criticized children's toys, such as Barbie and Ken dolls, for fuelling this obsession for thinness as these dolls are not representative of the range of human body shapes/sizes. While such dolls may be obvious culprits, children seem to be bombarded with body image messages that come from seemingly innocuous sources too, such as story books and fairy tales.

Researchers analysed twenty children's books, such as *Rapunzel* and *The Stinky Cheese Man*, for any kind of body image messages, including those regarding thinness or stereotypical, narrow definitions of beauty. While *The Stinky Cheese Man* and *Ginger* did not have these messages, the rest of the eighteen books did. In fact, *Rapunzel*, which is a popular story book, contained the highest number of such messages, such as the importance of physical attractiveness. Stereotypically defined attractive female characters or thin characters were depicted as sociable, kind, happy or successful. On the other hand, obesity was associated with negative traits in 20 per cent of these books.[12] No wonder five-year-olds are picking up the bias that thin is beautiful, while being overweight is bad.

Music lyrics

Exposure to music can be deliberate or incidental. It can be playing in the background when children go to malls or shops or when they attend celebrations. Music often blares out of players or radios in cars or buses. In addition, music transcends barriers of economic status and educational levels and can be heard playing in most homes.

A 2005 US study found that 85 per cent of the eight to eighteen years age group listen to music. The average amount of time spent listening to music daily increases with age from fifty-nine minutes spent by eight- to ten-year-olds, to two hours and twenty-four minutes spent by the fourteen to eighteen age group. The study also showed that 63 per cent of those who listen to music also use another media, such as the computer, or perform some other activity while listening to music.[13] The picture this finding brings to mind is of a young person with headphones on walking down the road, or cleaning his/her room, or even solving some mathematical problems, all while listening to music!

While research data regarding music consumption by Indian youth is not available, it is clear just by observing people that music forms a major part of a person's life, regardless of age. Young people in India have exposure and access to both music produced in India and abroad.

Music fulfils an important role, especially in an adolescent's life. It is used as a means to express individuality. Young people who are more in touch with their cultural roots, or are comfortable being viewed as traditional/conventional, may prefer to listen to classical music. On the other hand, young people who are more in touch with their rebellious side may seek out newer, alternative music genres. The majority of children who just want to fit in may follow whatever is most popular, whether it is Bollywood music or the Grammy award lists. Music, a common topic of conversation, allows young people to bond together. It is also used by young people as a tool for emotional expression. It can be uplifting if they are feeling low, it calms an agitated state of mind, and if one is in a party mood, it sets the scene for the party.

While exposure to music is nothing new and in itself is not a cause for concern, music lyrics are another story. Gone are the days of the innocent *Sound of Music* type of songs. Scholars report that the lyrics of songs today have become 'explicit, particularly with references to sex, drugs and violence'.[14] The American Academy of Paediatrics (AAP) has published a report that comprehensively reviews research on the impact of music, music lyrics and music videos on children and adolescents. According to the article, studies show that certain genres of music, including rap, rock, heavy metal and reggaeton, tend to talk often about sexual promiscuity, death, suicide and homicide. Some rap music, especially, is characterized by the presence of explicit sexual language, homophobia and hatred for women in the lyrics. Drugs, tobacco and alcohol use have also been glorified in these songs.[15] As for music specifically liked by teenagers, 'Researchers coded the content of 164 songs from 16 artists popular with teens. Overall, 15% of songs contained sexually degrading lyrics.'[16]

But we do not have to look at Western or English songs only—many of the current popular Bollywood songs or singers, such as Yo Yo Honey Singh, invariably talk about alcohol and sex, glorifying them: for example, 'chaar botal vodka', 'chhoti dress mein killer lagti meinu'. Many popular songs are set to catchy tunes that can be danced to, and one can often see children as young as two to three years old dancing to them.

The concern, then, is not only about the explicit messages that young people receive from such songs, but also about the exposure of children at younger ages to developmentally inappropriate and detrimental influences. Research has shown that even when children do not understand the exact meaning of the lyrics of a song, they are able to form an impression of what the song is trying to convey.[17]

The earlier mentioned AAP report[18] highlights some

worrying research findings. Studies indicate that young people who experience negative emotions when listening to any genre of music, prefer listening to more of such music. Hence, music may serve to reinforce negative emotions. In fact, one study found that children exposed to certain genres, such as heavy metal music, had more 'negative stereotyped attitudes' towards women than those who were exposed to classical music instead. Another study found that men who listened to songs that portray women in a negative manner viewed women in a more negative light, and acted more aggressively towards them.

Music lyrics also seem to have a direct impact on the sexual behaviour of young people. Research has shown that youth who listen to music with degrading sexual lyrics are likely to initiate sexual activity, including sexual intercourse, earlier than those who do not listen to such lyrics.[19] Therefore, while it may not be possible to establish direct cause-and-effect relationships between music lyrics and behaviour, it is clear that music lyrics can, and do, influence or reinforce attitudes and behaviour.

Music videos

In 2010, the American Psychological Association (APA) came out with a report on the sexualization of girls[20] based on different kinds of media research. According to the report, 'A recent analysis of the most popular music videos on Black Entertainment Television found sexual imagery in 84% of the videos; the two most frequently occurring sexual behaviours were sexual objectification and women dancing sexually. 71% of women in these videos were dressed in mildly provocative or provocative clothing or wore no clothing at all, compared with 35% of male characters.' Research mentioned in the report points out that the women who appear in most music videos do not sing or play any instrument but are featured as decorative sexual objects, posing and dancing in ways that focus on their bodies, body parts, facial features and sexual readiness. These findings are not restricted to pop or hip-hop videos; other genres, such as country music, also show a sexualized content.

According to the AAP report,[22] research shows that 'exposure to violence, sexual messages, sexual stereotypes, and use of substances of abuse in music videos might produce significant changes in the behaviours and attitudes of young viewers. As with popular music, the perception and the effect of music video messages on children and adolescents is related to the age and developmental and emotional stage of the viewer, as well as the level of exposure'. What this means is that young children may not understand the exact references and meaning of music videos, and a one-time exposure may not have any impact. However, for adolescents who are beginning to become aware of their sexuality and are curious about sexual topics, such videos become very significant sources of information. Messages received from such videos create the foundation for mistaken beliefs and assumptions about sex and sexuality, since impressions gathered at this age are absorbed without any critical analysis.

Research has also shown that music videos impact girls and boys in different ways. For girls, the major impact seems to be that music videos promote false stereotypes and reinforce the notion that weight and appearance are of great importance. The influence of such videos on boys is of equal, if not greater, concern. A study compared the impact of violent rap music videos or sexist videos on boys who were exposed to such videos versus those who were not. Boys who were exposed to such videos showed a greater inclination towards accepting violence in general, as well as violence specifically against women, and indicated the possibility of engaging in violent behaviour themselves in the future. Studies have also found that watching music videos, such as on MTV, is associated with greater acceptance of premarital sex. In addition, mostly watching rap videos has been associated with greater promiscuity and alcohol and drug use.[23]

Television

A major form of entertainment for children in India is television. On average, Indian children watch between one to three hours of television a day.[24] Research on the effect of television viewing has been carried out since the 1960s, and concerns since then have been raised about the relationship between television viewing and aggression.[25] Recent studies have shown that television viewing can have a major impact on the social, emotional and cognitive development of children, with both positive and negative effects.

While some television programmes can be informative and educational, such as the *National Geographic* shows on wildlife or ecology, a lot of the programmes are pure entertainment. Shows like *Friends*, which are actually meant for young adults, are often watched by young teenagers. 'Television exposes children to adult sexual behaviours in ways that portray these actions as normal and risk-free, sending the message that because these behaviours are frequent, "everybody does it". Sex between unmarried partners is shown 24 times more often than sex between spouses, while sexually transmitted infections and unwanted pregnancy are rarely mentioned.'[26]

Studies show that the frequency of sexual references on television has increased in the past decade and have become increasingly explicit. Studies on the effects of this content, while scarce, suggest that 'adolescents who rely heavily on television for information about sexuality will have high standards of female beauty and will believe that premarital and extramarital intercourse with multiple partners is acceptable. They are unlikely to learn about the need for contraceptives as a form of protection against pregnancy or disease'.[27]

Films

Children have always watched films, animated or otherwise, based on fairy tales, books and Disney stories. A study analysed twenty-five popular classic and new videos/animated movies for children,[28] including *Lion King*, *Cinderella* and *101 Dalmatians*, among others. The study found that these films, on average, contained 8.7 out of ten body-related messages, which included a narrow definition of physical beauty, thin is 'good', obese is 'bad', lacking physical/facial features that match the narrow definition of beauty is 'bad', and other such messages. The number of these messages was much higher than those present in children's books.

The highest number of body-related messages was found in *Cinderella* and *Little Mermaid*. *ET* was the children's video that carried the least number of such messages, but did have one. While 72 per cent of the children's videos placed an emphasis on physical attractiveness, associating 'thin' with desirable traits, 84 per cent of the videos had content associating female physical attractiveness with kindness, sociability, happiness and success. In 60 per cent of the videos, which were mostly classic stories, one character's love for another was based on his or her physical attractiveness. In 56 per cent of the videos, male characters considered attractive had slim or muscular figures. Being obese was associated with negative traits in 64 per cent of the videos.

Children now seem to prefer cartoon films or videos to books as the primary source of entertainment—this increases their exposure to such body image messages, which raises various concerns. Research has shown that regular exposure to images of people with very thin bodies is correlated with the desire to be thin among children and adolescents.[29] It is likely that watching films with slim actors gets young children to believe in the stereotype of thin being the ideal.

Also, frequently being exposed to the 'thinness' message seems to reinforce the idea that being thin is the norm, leading to the erroneous belief that a healthy weight or overweight is an exception. It also promotes the misconception that to have positive personality traits or to be successful, happy and loved, a specific criteria of facial features and body shape or size has to be met. Hence, seeds are sown early for children to develop eating and body image-related disorders.

As far as movies for adolescents are concerned, researchers point out that they almost always show nude people and sexual intercourse scenes. These movies, such as the *American Pie* series, also tend to present distorted views of romance and adolescent sexuality.[30] Results from a longitudinal study suggest that exposure to sex in movies may promote sexual risk-taking in adolescents. Such exposure influences adolescents by both modifying their sexual behaviour and by accelerating the normal rise in sensation-seeking that occurs at this age.[31]

Video games

Ubiquitous now, video games have become increasingly popular in the past couple of decades. From gaming stations to cellphones, almost all interactive devices have games available on them. Children are attracted to video games because they are highly stimulating and absorbing. Since they have several levels built into them, children of all ages, even adults, can play these games. They can be played alone, with other people, offline or online while also interacting with other video games' players in real time. The other players may be known or unknown individuals.

Children Now, a US based organization, asserts that these games 'often contain characters that epitomise stereotypical gender roles and also may contain sexually explicit content, despite ratings that are approved for children'. They point out that 'Male characters are more likely to engage in physical aggression, while female characters are severely under-represented (only 16% of all characters); and often wear revealing clothing, and/or have a nurturing role.'[32]

Many children play video games on a daily basis. Considering the fact that children spend vast amounts of time playing video games, such exposure is likely to have a negative impact on the self-image of girls. Not only that, it also warps the way boys view girls and negatively impacts the expectations they have from girls or women in the future.[33]

Advertising

The media often uses sexual content to sell a variety of unrelated products. 'Women are featured as "decorations" in ads (e.g., shown standing seductively next to a car to enhance the image of the car), their major purpose is to be looked at. They are treated as appendages to the product rather than as active consumers or users of the product.'[34] In addition, the women shown tend to be thin, physically attractive and partially clothed.

Researchers note that this is also true for children's advertising. Sexual imagery is common and girls, especially, are inappropriately sexualized when they are objectified and portrayed in provocative poses.[35] Ads often use a star popular with teens and preteens and present her in highly sexualized poses. Some explicitly play up innocence as sexy, as in one of the Skechers shoes' 'naughty and nice' ads that featured Christina Aguilera dressed as a schoolgirl in pigtails, with her shirt unbuttoned, licking a lollipop.[36]

The worry is that this kind of advertising 'may promote an ideal of attractiveness. Young girls and boys see sexualized images of girls in magazines, which may affect their views of body image and sexuality. Sexualized images in advertising also increase sexual content exposure in general, which can have negative effects on developing children'.[37] Advertising often blurs the line between who is sexually mature and who is not. The use of text, such as 'hot chick', 'hot tot', 'flirty baby', on children's clothing and 'print advertisements that portray women as little girls, with pigtails and ruffles, in adult sexual poses', all contribute towards sexualizing childhood.[38]

Impact of Hyper-sexualization: The Body Image Mess

'Sex and sexuality in the media are widespread, even those programs that are targeted at children. Despite recommendations from health officials, children may be exposed to up to 53 hours of entertainment media per week.'[39] There is, therefore, an onslaught of sexualized media images that children are exposed to. While girls are affected by the way the media portrays girls, they are also influenced indirectly by the way women are sexualized by the media.

The media sexualization of women and girls, therefore, teaches girls that women are sexual objects.[40] This results in self-objectification by girls, which further leads to girls developing eating disorders, low self-esteem and depression. Sexual objectification also interferes with the healthy sexual development of children and reduces their sexual understanding.[41]

'Although the media can be used for sexual education and other types of learning, the majority of the effects of sexual content in the media are negative. Portrayals of sexual activity and sexuality are often inaccurate and unrealistic, and they do not depict healthy relationships or sexual activity. Gender roles are often stereotypical and emphasis is placed on physical attractiveness, even in young children. This can affect children's understanding of sexual health and sexuality, gender role construction, stereotypical thinking, self-image, and sexual activity.'[42] Scholars point out that 'Females are especially prone to the normalization of sexual promiscuity, which heightens their risk of being victims of unwanted sexual violence and of sexually transmitted diseases'.[43]

It is clear that the modern socio-cultural obsession with body shapes and sizes impacts children and adults alike. What this means is that the child's peer group and the family is also fed the same media diet. Everyone falls into the same trap of trying to achieve the unachievable media-defined ideal. In fact, research has related body dissatisfaction, obsession with weight-control and dieting disorders to the influence exerted by different kinds of media.[44]

Research indicates that if a child is teased by peers about weight issues and the family's focus is on weight, even if it is in the form of encouragement to lose weight, it leads to the child developing a dissatisfaction with his/her body image. Research has further identified specific parental behaviours that have a significant impact on children, especially adolescent girls. These behaviours include parental complaints about their own weight, the mother's dieting pattern, the mother's comments about her daughter's weight, and specific encouragement to lose weight. All these parental behaviours are associated with adolescent girls trying to lose weight in an attempt to attain the media-defined ideal shape and size.[45]

The biggest concern that researchers and practitioners express is regarding the consequences of children's dissatisfaction with their body image. At the age of twelve–thirteen years, girls often gain fat tissue and appear to be the furthest from this ideal body shape/size. At this age, a mismatch between socio-cultural expectations regarding physical appearance and the adolescent's own body can lead many young girls to develop a negative body image. This, in turn, translates to low self-esteem and self-oriented perfectionism, which prompts an adolescent to pursue an unachievable, unrealistic shape/size. Extreme diets and extreme exercise regimens are adopted, but as neither of these interventions promotes a sustainable, healthy lifestyle, weight gain reoccurs. For some people, the yo-yo cycle of weight gain and loss continues.

Research also indicates that, sometimes, adolescents fall into the trap of thinking that fixing their weight will also bring about happiness and wellness. Such beliefs can result in disorders such as anorexia and bulimia, which can be life-threatening conditions.[46] Both anorexia and bulimia can affect girls as well as boys. Anorexia nervosa is a condition where a person is obsessed with reducing body weight. Often, despite being slim, individuals affected by this disorder can continue to severely limit their food intake and/or exercise excessively to the extent that they become severely underweight, girls experience irregular menstruation, and individuals may even die due to associated health complications. Bulimia is a disorder in which individuals go through a binge–purge cycle where they may eat or overeat, and then, make themselves vomit or take laxatives in an attempt to control their weight. Other than weight loss, this condition can lead to health issues related to a loss of electrolytes and complications, including permanent damage to the oesophagus.

Another disorder that can develop due to a negative body image is body dysmorphic disorder. Individuals suffering from it are obsessed with their physical appearance and believe they have significant flaws in their physical appearance, even when there are none. This condition can also develop in adolescence and last for a lifetime, causing individuals to lead restricted lives and go through innumerable procedures, including cosmetic surgery, to fix the perceived or imagined flaw.[47]

Dissatisfaction with one's body image also tends to get carried into adulthood and influences one's sexuality. Even when young people reach a healthy weight, they are unable to shake off the dissatisfaction they feel with their bodies. A lack of comfort and confidence with one's body translates into a lack of comfort with one's sexuality and ultimately, as adults, intimate relationships are negatively affected.

Chapter 6

CHILD SEXUAL ABUSE

*When we talk with our children about sexual abuse,
we are not only taking a proactive step toward protecting them,
we are building our relationship with them—grounded in
honesty and trust. It's a win-win situation.*
—Carolyn Byers Ruch

Child sexual abuse in India is rampant. It is very likely that today's newspaper would have reported at least one case of child sexual abuse. The latest official figures regarding prevalence of child sexual abuse in India are based on a study conducted by the Ministry of Women and Child Development in 2007.[1] The study reports that out of a total of 2,211 respondents, 42 per cent had experienced one or more forms of child sexual abuse; 48 per cent of the boys and 39 per cent of the girls who participated in this study reported sexual abuse. The study also found that the prevalence of sexual abuse was higher in children who belonged to upper and middle class families as compared to lower or lower middle class families.

Now, whatever be the exact and most current prevalence rates or patterns, the fact remains that all parents worry about child sexual abuse. And while we do need to think about preventing our children from becoming victims, we also need to prevent our children from becoming abusers. The way we can do this is by educating ourselves, going beyond the newspaper reports, and looking more closely at the dynamics of abuse.

Let's first start with the definition of child sexual abuse. Any sexual act that an adult does to a child constitutes child sexual abuse. The adult may use violence or threats in order to sexually abuse a child or be very gentle and persuasive. In fact, the most common methods employed by child abusers are enticement, rewards, misuse of authority or misrepresentation of what is happening.[2] Whether the child does or does not give consent to the sexual act is immaterial.[3]

Mic Hunter[4] describes various behaviours that can be defined as sexually abusive. These behaviours include those that are legally defined as sexually abusive in India, as well as more subtle behaviours that are not part of the legal definition. Though many of these behaviours may not involve touch and may not come within the legal definition, they are sexual in nature and constitute an abuse of authority, power and trust that an adult holds over a child. The following is a list of such sexually abusive behaviours:

- An adult sexually touching a child
- Making the child touch the adult sexually
- Photographing the child for sexual purposes
- Sexualized talk with a child
- Showing the child pornographic material or making it available to him/her
- Making fun of or ridiculing the child's sexual development, preferences or organs
- Exposing his/her genitals to the child for sexual gratification
- Masturbating or otherwise being sexual in front of the child
- Voyeurism involving a child
- Forcing extremely rigid rules on a child's dress, whether it be very revealing or very modest
- Stripping to hit or spank, or getting sexual excitement out of hitting a child

- Verbal or emotional abuse of the child, which is of a sexual nature
- Making the child be sexual with animals
- Engaging the child in prostitution
- Making the child witness others being sexually abused

Sexual contact between an older child and a younger child can also be termed as sexual abuse if there is a significant difference in size, age or developmental level, which leaves one child incapable of giving informed consent.[5] For example, a same age or perhaps even younger child may sexually abuse an older child who has developmental challenges or disabilities, which leave him/her incapable of giving informed consent. 'Children with disabilities are three times more likely to be abused than children without disabilities. In particular, children with intellectual disabilities are five times more likely to be abused.'[6] Hence, children with disabilities are the most vulnerable to sexual abuse by other children and adults.

All children, regardless of gender, can become victims of sexual abuse. 'Girls and young women face an increased vulnerability to violence because they are both female and a child and are therefore doubly disadvantaged by both gender and age discrimination. If they are indigenous or disabled or face another form of discrimination, this vulnerability is further exacerbated.'[7]

At the same time, boys have to deal with the notion of 'masculinity' and homophobia, which makes it even more difficult for them to disclose experiences of sexual abuse. The experience of being passive and helpless in the face of the abuse and the fact that most abusers are male 'creates powerful barriers to male victim/survivors of child sexual abuse disclosing their experiences to others, accepting their experience as one that may have had a formative influence on their lives, and healing from the trauma of the abuse'.[8]

Secrecy and denial of the abuse by the abuser are the hallmarks of child sexual abuse. These aspects have a role to play in the way abuse occurs and also on the impact the abuse has on the child. Most often, child sexual abuse occurs within one of two contexts: the abuser either deliberately and in a preplanned manner 'grooms' or forges a sense of familiarity/relationship with the child for the specific purpose of sexually abusing the child. Or, the abuser misuses an existing relationship with the child to sexually abuse him/her. Force is rarely required or used in child sexual abuse.[9]

The message of secrecy around the abuse that the abuser communicates to the child, either directly or indirectly, often leaves the child feeling confused or unsure about his/her role in the abuse. It is for this reason that the child often does not complain to anyone about the abuse. Sexual abuse is, therefore, discovered much after the events have occurred—when the child later realizes that the experience was abuse and only then discloses it to someone. For many children, child sexual abuse remains a secret they keep forever out of a mistaken sense of shame, loyalty towards the abuser, fear that he/she will be disbelieved, blamed or held responsible for the abuse, and in some cases, fear of reprisal from the abuser.

Characteristics of a Child Sex Abuser

Adult child sex abusers

People who sexually abuse children can belong to any gender (though most are men), age, class, caste, religion, profession or educational level. They can be teachers, doctors, policemen, watchmen, drivers, businessmen, coaches, spiritual leaders or preachers of different faiths. They can be deeply religious, non-religious or agnostic. They may be very successful in their careers or just getting by. They may be married and have children or grandchildren of their own, or be single. They may be very sociable and confident people or be loners and appear socially inept. In short, there is no one profile of a child sex abuser and it is difficult to tell whether a person is or is not an abuser.

What is common amongst child sex abusers is that they tend to not have any kind of psychiatric condition and appear as 'normal' as you and me. They are most likely to be people known to the child, such as neighbours, relatives, caretakers or other people the child interacts with on a regular basis. In addition, while many use the excuse that they themselves were victims of child sexual abuse, research in this field indicates that only about 20–30 per cent of adult as well as adolescent child sex abusers have a history of being sexually abused.

Researchers further point out that younger children who have sexually abused other children seem to have the highest chance of being victims of sexual abuse themselves. This likelihood decreases with older children and adolescents who abuse. Interestingly, research has found that adults who commit sexual offences against adults have a far higher degree of psychopathic traits than those who sexually offend against children. It is important to note that child sex abusers who have psychopathic traits are most likely to continue to sexually abuse children and be violent, even after they have been caught and undergone treatment.[10]

Researchers and practitioners in this field differentiate between paedophiles and non-paedophilic child sex abusers. The primary difference between the two is that paedophiles prefer to interact sexually with children rather than with adults.

Hence, paedophiles may not have any adult sexual relationships, nor be interested in adult sexual relationships. The other child sex abusers turn to children as a matter of convenience or availability, or it can be 'an expression of power, compulsiveness, a desire for control, or an act of vengeance, which often comes masked as an act of love'.[11] Such child sex abusers are the ones who may be married or may marry in the future, or have other adult sexual relationships. All abusers primarily use children's innocence, gullibility and lack of power and authority to get their own sexual needs met.

Child/adolescent child sex abusers

Children are sometimes sexually abused by other children or teenagers. For legal and, most importantly, developmental reasons, the sexually problematic behaviour shown by children under twelve years of age (prepubertal children) is put in a different category from sexually abusive behaviour shown by adolescents. The reason for this is that while the behaviour shown by prepubertal children may be sexual in nature, the intention and motivation to engage in such behaviours is not. The sexual behaviours prepubertal children show are not related to the sex drive or sexual gratification, in the way that they are for adolescents or adults. 'Prepubertal children simply do not experience sexual arousal and drives comparable to those of adults or adolescents.'[12]

Prepubertal children may show problematic sexual behaviour that can be placed in one of three categories: inappropriate conduct, sexually intrusive behaviour, or sexually aggressive behaviour. Children who show such behaviour may be boys or girls. In fact, many preschool children with sexual behaviour problems have been reported to be girls. Amongst prepubertal children who show problematic sexual behaviour, the most common age group is preschool children. The problematic actions they engage in can either be 'self-focused', such as excessive masturbation, or 'other-focused', such as making sexual remarks and gestures to others. Some children may show sexually intrusive behaviour, which includes unplanned, impulsive and non-aggressive sexual conduct.

A minority of children show sexual behaviours that are a serious concern primarily due to their use of force, threats, coercion or aggression, which accompanies their sexually inappropriate behaviour. Preschool children who engage in such aggressive behaviour tend to have themselves suffered child maltreatment or family violence, and also show other kinds of psychological problems.[13]

An explanation for why young children may exhibit sexually problematic behaviour is that they do not have very well developed thinking abilities and have limited ways of coping with stressful situations. In such instances, excessive masturbation or thumbsucking, may be engaged in by children as a way to self-soothe or make themselves feel better. As children grow older, their ability to think and cognitively handle situations gets better; therefore, they are able to cope with emotionally stressful situations in more acceptable ways.

It is also important to remember here that when such young children do engage in sexual behaviour with other children, it is not with either the intention or ability to pre-plan and 'groom' the victim. Young children misbehave because they are much more self-focused and do not have an ability to understand other people's perspectives or experiences, or even understand fully the concept of causes and consequences. In addition, short attention spans and limited impulse control are hallmarks of childhood.

Research also shows that children who engage in more

sexually aggressive behaviours typically come from family environments that are more stressful, and also show more general behaviour problems and emotional problems than other children. Children who show non-aggressive sexual behaviour problems also tend to have undergone extensive abuse or neglect at home.[14]

Research shows that adolescents who sexually assault others tend to abuse younger children more than they assault adults. While such young people vary considerably in terms of their personality characteristics, mental health issues and family backgrounds, there are some common characteristics that researchers have identified. Compared to other teenagers, adolescents who sexually abuse children are found to have weak social skills, non-sexual behaviour problems, learning disabilities, depression and impulse control issues. (However, their level of behaviour problems and learning disabilities are not more significant than those of non-offending teenagers.)

Researchers have also found some differences between adolescents who sexually abuse younger children versus those who offend against children their age. Adolescents who molest younger children seem more submissive, dependent and withdrawn; they also show a tendency to belittle themselves. On the other hand, teenagers who rape peers tend to be older, more socially competent, engaged in more peer sexual activity and show more conduct problems, that is, they engage in behaviours that are illegal. In general, compared to adult child sex abusers, adolescents who molest children engage in fewer abusive behaviours, offend over shorter periods of time, and less frequently involve penile penetration.[15]

When one looks at the family background of teenagers who sexually abuse others, one finds that their parents typically show a higher level of alcohol or substance abuse, and their mothers tend to suffer from depression. The overall family background of most, but not all, of these adolescents tends to be at extremes. On the one extreme, their family environment may be very chaotic with parents who are unable or unwilling to exert parental authority and provide appropriate supervision, or they have parents who are outright neglectful and not interested in the child. On the other extreme, such children have parents who tend to be overly strict, punitive, extremely rigid about rules and overly controlling/intrusively involved.

It is important to note that most adolescents, especially those who have been through treatment, do not go on to perpetrate sexual offences as adults, unless they get into other criminal activity, have antisocial tendencies or show traits of a psychopath. Psychopathic traits include 'emotional shallowness, insincerity, callousness, interpersonal exploitation, lack of guilt or remorse, impulsiveness, pathological lying, proneness towards violence, and persistent violation of social norms'.[16]

Sibling abuse and incest are the least spoken about kinds of sexual abuse that children undergo. Sibling abuse often occurs due to the ease of access, availability and the ability to exploit the fact that a relationship already exists between the victim and abuser. In fact, it is the relationship that makes it the most difficult for victims to speak up about sexual abuse by a sibling. 'Sibling sexual offending has received limited empirical attention, despite estimates that approximately half of all adolescent-perpetrated sexual offences involve a sibling victim.'[17] It is important to remember, though, that mutual sexual exploration out of curiosity and sibling abuse are two separate things.

Incest of any kind is not 'normal' and exists when families become dysfunctional in significant ways: parents undergo conflict or there is a great imbalance of power or violence in the parents' relationship, and siblings are left with inadequate or no supervision and nurturing. Research, in fact, indicates that adolescents who sexually abused a sibling (versus those who abused a non-sibling) were more likely to have been sexually abused themselves and been exposed to domestic violence and pornography.[18]

What all this means is that there are family-based factors which have a huge impact on the development of children and teenagers. In fact, these factors seem to play a significant role in children and teenagers becoming child sex abusers. To sum up, the problematic family characteristics are: the presence of domestic violence or extreme conflict/power imbalance between the parents, mental health issues of the parents, including alcohol/substance abuse and depression, the parents' inability or unwillingness to offer appropriate supervision and nurturance to children and teenagers, extremely strict or punitive parenting, and exposure to sexual abuse and pornography.

Impact of Child Sexual Abuse on Victims and Survivors

Short-term impact

Like there is no one picture of a child sex abuser, there is no one picture of a child who has been sexually abused. Research shows that children who have suffered maltreatment, neglect or abuse of any kind, especially at home, show similar symptoms and cannot be distinguished.[19] This means that one cannot tell whether a child is showing problematic behaviour due to physical abuse, sexual abuse, or neglect. In addition, children who grow up in homes where they have witnessed domestic violence on a regular basis can show the same set of symptoms as a child who has been sexually abused.

In fact, not all children go through all the symptoms and there is no single syndrome or set of symptoms that children who have been sexually abused show. Research shows that other factors, such as support for the child, especially from parents or other significant adults, can reduce the short- and long-term impact of child sexual abuse. The impact of abuse can also vary—this means that a pre-adolescent child who does not show any symptoms immediately after the abuse can experience difficulties when she enters puberty, or even much later as an adult, when she forms intimate relationships.

Specific to sexual abuse, the most common problems that children undergo as a result of such abuse are experiencing post-traumatic stress disorder (PTSD) symptoms and sexual behaviour problems.[20] For example, nightmares and/or other sleep difficulties may increase; the child may suffer from flashbacks regarding the abuse or experience intrusive thoughts/memories of the abuse. The child may also show sexual knowledge, language, and/or behaviours that are inappropriate for his/her age.[21]

Some children who have been sexually abused may also show more general symptoms of psychological distress, such as withdrawn behaviour, anger outbursts, anxiety or depression.[22] In addition, children who feel guilty or blame themselves for the abuse also develop lower self-esteem and undergo depression and anxiety. Guilt is also related with higher levels of PTSD symptoms.[23]

Children who have been abused sometimes express their emotional distress through physical conditions and complain of chronic abdominal pain, headaches, anal or pelvic pain, vocal chord dysfunction, pseudo-seizures, fibromyalgia, enuresis (urinary incontinence), encopresis (faecal impaction or soiling), or other psychosomatic conditions (that is, physical complaints for which an actual physical cause cannot be found). All these symptoms are not imaginary nor is the child pretending. These conditions are real and arise as a result of the body's response to stress and psychological pain.[24]

It is important to remember that most of the above signs are not symptoms specific to sexual abuse and some children who have undergone other kinds of emotionally traumatic experiences, such as being in an accident, experiencing the death of a loved one, witnessing violence, or being severely bullied may also show some of these symptoms. At the same time, some children who have experienced sexual abuse may show no effects/symptoms whatsoever of having ever been abused.

Adolescents who have been sexually abused may show somewhat different negative effects of the abuse than younger children who have been sexually abused. Adolescents who experience sexual abuse may show self-esteem issues, depression and self-harm behaviour, including cutting, suicidal thoughts or behaviour, school or academic problems, conflict with authorities, early sexual behaviour and eating disorders. Research shows that girls who experience a high level of shame associated with abuse also experience much lower self-esteem, more severe depression and a more intense manifestation of PTSD symptoms.[25]

However, not all adolescents show the above-mentioned negative effects or need treatment. Adolescents are particularly sensitive about going through psychotherapy as they may see it as a punishment, especially if they feel the abuser has been able to escape without undergoing treatment or other consequences. They may also view therapy as 'another unwelcome exposure of their most embarrassing secrets'.[26]

Long-term impact

'Childhood sexual abuse is associated with a broad array of adverse consequences for survivors throughout their lifetime.

As a result of more rigorous research studies in this field our understanding of the impacts of childhood sexual abuse is becoming more nuanced and a robust body of research evidence now clearly demonstrates the link between child sexual abuse and a spectrum of adverse mental health, social, sexual, interpersonal and behavioural as well as physical health consequences. To date, the strongest links have been found between child sexual abuse and the presence of depression, alcohol and substance abuse, eating disorders for women survivors, and anxiety-related disorders for male survivors. An increased risk of re-victimisation of survivors has also been demonstrated consistently for both men and women survivors. Some more recent research has also revealed a link between child sexual abuse and personality, psychotic and schizophrenic disorders, as well as a heightened risk for suicide ideation and suicidal behaviour.'[27]

Further, 'Many male victim/survivors of child sexual abuse are aware of, and troubled by, the widespread promotion of what has been called the "victim-to-offender" discourse.'[28] While research shows that it is neither automatic nor inevitable that male children who have been sexually abused will end up sexually abusing other children,[29] the idea does have a significant impact on male survivors of child sexual abuse. Male survivors often express a fear that they themselves may end up sexually abusing their own children, which affects their ability to bond with them. Such survivors are often uncomfortable with touching or displaying affection for their children. Some male survivors also tend to be anxious as parents, and overprotective of their children.[30]

Prevention

Often parents and schools do not want to introduce sex and sexuality related information to children because there is a huge discomfort with the topic. Fears range from thinking that doing so will take away a child's innocence to finding it embarrassing to discuss or explain what sex is, especially if the child asks the dreaded question about what it means. The fact is that one can teach children how to watch out for anyone trying to sexually abuse them without ever using the word 'sex'.

Children as young as two years old begin to have a strong sense of ownership and control over their bodies; getting a child of this age to bathe or to change his/her diaper requires their cooperation and assent. If parents communicate a sense of respect and affirm the child's control over his/her own body, the child will develop a sense of ownership over his/her body. For example, ask for his/her assent before changing a diaper or giving a bath. The same approach can be used when demonstrating affection. This means allowing the child to decide if she/he wants to give a relative a hug or a kiss and respecting his/her decision to say 'No'. It also means getting the child's permission before picking him up and hugging or kissing him. This in no way implies that one must stop hugging and kissing children. In fact, hug and kisses are powerful ways by which a sense of acceptance, love, affection, safety and security are communicated to a child.

Touch is sometimes more reassuring and comforting than words. But since certain kinds of touch are harmful, it is important to help children develop their own ability to distinguish between 'good touch' and 'bad touch'. To be able to refuse touch that is intrusive, inappropriate or unwelcome requires that the child be given the power to choose.

Most children are abused by someone they know and trust.[31] At the same time, as a parent you may not want to inculcate a sense of mistrust in your child or make them fearful of everyone in their world. Hence, instead of focusing on people—strangers or otherwise—who can harm them, you can focus on behaviour.

It is important to convey to children very clearly that certain acts or behaviours are not okay. Children are quite used to being told by parents about different kinds of behaviour, especially those that the parents consider undesirable. For example, children are often told at school and at home not to fight or hit anyone. In the same vein, they can be taught that they can touch their own private body parts in the privacy of their own rooms or bathrooms when no one is present. However, touching the private areas of others, or touching one's own private areas in the presence of others is not acceptable behaviour. Neither is a person of any age allowed to touch the child's private parts. You can also tell them that anyone who indulges in such behaviour or asks them to do the same, whether a child or an adult, is behaving inappropriately and should be asked to stop.

There are many ways to reinforce this information and you will need to talk about this many times and in different ways with children, just as you do about not hitting and fighting. For example, young children, aged four to six years, are often curious and peep into the bathroom when other children or adults are using it. It is important to intervene at these times and remind children that peeping in or watching someone undress is unacceptable behaviour.

As children grow older, at ages six and seven, and confront different kinds of behaviour, including mean or violent conduct, in the playground or in school, you can talk about the fact that sometimes people, even those the child knows, can behave in a hurtful or harmful manner. At this point, you can expand on the earlier teaching and specifically tell children that sometimes some individuals, children or adults, may try to touch their private parts or ask them to touch theirs or ask them/themselves to become naked. One can reiterate at this point that such behaviour is not acceptable at all and if someone behaves in this manner with the child, he/she should come and tell you. They can also tell the person that you have told them that this kind of conduct is not okay.

Teach children to take care of their own private parts (that is, bathing, wiping, washing after bathroom use) so they don't have to rely on adults or older children for help.[32] Around the age of six years, most children can learn to wash/wipe themselves after using the bathroom. They can also bathe themselves and wear their own clothes, especially if the pants or other lowers have elastic waistbands.

Encourage your children to become independent in this way so that they do not need the help of anyone else. This also forges an even stronger sense of privacy in terms of their body so that they will then know if their privacy is being invaded. At this time, you can also inform children clearly that adults and older children never need help with their private body parts (for example, bathing or going to the bathroom).[33]

A hallmark of child sexual abuse is the misuse of the concept of 'secrets'. As abusers often use the concept of keeping a secret to lure and bind children to an abusive relationship, it is important to explain to children the difference between 'surprises' and 'secrets'.[34]

Surprises, such as surprise parties or birthday gifts, are okay because they are not kept secret for long and can be shared with some people. However, secrets are those that the child is supposed to keep forever. Secrets are not okay.[35] You could decide who other than you is a trusted adult and tell the child that he/she needs to tell either you or this trusted person about any secret that anyone asks them to keep. You can also tell them that it is okay to refuse to keep a secret and that anything that makes them feel scared, uncomfortable or confused is probably not a good secret to keep. You can also give them permission to tell anyone they trust if they feel this way.[36]

Make it known to the other adults in your child's life, especially those who take care of the child in your absence and especially if your child has a disability, what 'good touch' and 'bad touch' is. It is sometimes uncomfortable to talk to adults about this topic but talking about it is what can keep the child safe. Child sexual abuse exists and carries on due to the silence that shrouds it.

Explain to the adults involved in your child's life that the concept of secrets can make children vulnerable. Request them not to ask children to keep secrets. Make it clear to them that children have the right to request privacy or say 'no'.[37]

Stay involved in your child's life. Keep an allotted stretch of time each day to communicate with your children so that they can share what they did, what they experienced and who they interacted with. Get to know who, whether adult or children, your children engage with, what kind of activities/games they play, and the places they visit. This is particularly important for children in the age group of eight to twelve years who are beginning to move around independently, are not as closely supervised as younger children, but who do not feel as confident as older teenagers in asserting themselves.

Be alert. Watch out for any inappropriate behaviour demonstrated by children or adults. Intervene if this is the case and in no uncertain terms tell them to stop engaging in such behaviour.[38]

Be aware of any special relationships that your child may develop, especially with a much younger or much older child or adult. Encourage such relationships to be conducted in your presence, under supervision or in the presence of others. Encourage openness around these relationships; encourage your children to share what they talk about and what they do with their 'special' friend. Share the 'no secrets' rule with your child and the 'special' friend.

Encourage non-sexist attitudes and behaviour in the family. For example: give power, responsibility and privileges equally to male and female siblings; assign household tasks fairly, and discourage sexist jokes and sexist put-downs.[39] Encourage all family members, including siblings, to respect each other's privacy and personal space. Support your son's and daughter's efforts to establish their privacy and personal space.

If you are an adult who harbours sexual thoughts and feelings towards children, you need to stop and think. Child sexual abuse can never be justified and you can access help to prevent yourself from acting on inappropriate impulses. Please contact a psychotherapist or psychologist who has the necessary training and experience in this area. You may also be able to access help on the Internet.

Intervention

'Trust your instincts! If you feel uneasy about leaving a child with someone, don't do it. If you're concerned about possible sexual abuse, ask questions.'[40]

If you suspect that your child or a child you know may have been or is currently being sexually abused, it is important to talk to the child and ask him or her. Due to the confusing nature of abuse, the involvement of a known person and the element of secrecy that is often employed by the abuser, children rarely complain of sexual abuse.

Often, children realize that what they are experiencing or what they have experienced in the past is abuse only when they attend a talk at school on sexuality and abuse. When Sheila, a ten-year-old girl, attended a session on 'good touch' and 'bad touch' at school, she started crying. On being asked by the teacher what had upset her, she shared that her older brother had been abusing her. Similarly, sixteen-year-old Aadya seemed quite upset after her teacher conducted a session on sex, sexuality and abuse. She finally confided in a friend who encouraged her to speak with her teacher about the abuse.

The magic words or actions that reduce, minimize or erase the effects of child sexual abuse are belief and support. Research has found that when the parent, especially the mother, reacts to the child's disclosure of abuse by believing the child's report completely and showing absolute support, the child usually does not end up suffering from any major long-term effects of abuse.[41] Therefore, family relationships and the home environment, in general, and the family's reaction to the abuse, in particular, determine how well the child will recover from the abuse experience.

If this support does not come from the parents but comes from another adult, such as a grandparent or teacher, even that sense of support and understanding helps the child feel better and he/she is less likely to then develop behaviour problems.[42] A common way in which children express their emotional distress is by displaying problematic behaviour, which should alert the parent.

Research has also found that it helps children recover well from the abuse experience when they do not take on any blame or responsibility for the abuse.[43] Parents and other significant adults play a crucial role in helping the child do so. To achieve this you can tell your child very clearly that he/she is not to be blamed for the abuse and that whatever steps he/she took were okay. Sometimes, children blame themselves for not being able to escape or 'allowing' the abuser to abuse.[44] The fact is that the child does not have the power to prevent or stop the abuse. All children are taught to obey adults and just the sheer size difference is intimidating.[45]

Avoid statements like 'I told you not to visit their house!' or 'Why did you accept sweets from him when I told you not to!' Do not doubt what the child is telling you by saying, 'But how is that possible? I was with you all the time.' If anyone else says any of these things, stand by your child and reiterate that you believe him/her completely.

It is also important to communicate to the child that he/she did a brave thing by telling you. Disclosing abuse is one of the most difficult things to do because of the fear of being blamed, disbelieved or punished. There is often also a strong feeling of shame associated with being sexually abused. It is crucial that in your interaction with the child, you do not let the child feel any shame or guilt.

Moreover, in the long-term, it is beneficial for the child to know that though he/she was a powerless 'victim' in the context of the abuse, they could eventually 'do' something by telling you or someone else about it. You can also apologize to the child for not realizing how vulnerable he/she was and assure him/her that you now take responsibility to ensure that the abuser will not abuse again. It is important to remember child sexual abuse occurs because of adults, not because of children.

Friends are very important sources of support and influence, but they can also lead the child astray. Helping the child stay away from alcohol, drugs and peers who are engaged in deviant activities will lead to positive outcomes.[46] In addition, encouraging the child to pursue any area they are strongly interested in, such as academics or sports, will also help. An activity that the child enjoys and which provides a focus as well as an experience of task competence or a sense of accomplishment/success will help him/her build self-esteem and confidence.

Special Note

Many organizations and resources are available on the Internet that provide information to help parents protect their children and teenagers from sexual abuse. There are also several organizations that provide psychotherapy and support services to victims and survivors of child sexual abuse. As mentioned earlier, children who have special needs are the most vulnerable to sexual abuse. The following are some Internet resources that parents of children with disabilities could use in their effort to protect their children from sexual abuse:

- http://kc.vanderbilt.edu/kennedy_files/ProtectingChildrenwithDisabilitiesfromSexualAssaultAParentsGuide.pdf
- http://www.stopitnow.org/ohc-content/for-parents-of-children-with-disabilities
- https://www.autismspeaks.org/family-services/autism-safety-project/sexual-abuse

Chapter 7

WHAT PARENTS CAN DO

The most important gift adults can give children is self-esteem. When adults show children that they value and love them unconditionally, children can withstand the perils of childhood and adolescence with fewer scars and traumas. Self-esteem is a universal vaccine that can immunize a youngster from eating problems, body image distortion, exercise abuse, and many other problems. Providing self-esteem is the responsibility of both parents. Girls especially need support and validation from their fathers.
—Dr Paula Levine

It goes without saying that not all children or adults look the same. Our racial and ethnic background and a complex interplay of genes, which we have no control over, determine what we look like. Each child who is born is beautiful, and each child deserves to feel so.

Children do not inherently feel more or less beautiful than their peers; it is only when they start receiving messages from the family, friends or the media that they begin to compare themselves with these messages and, eventually, with each other. This is when a sense of dissatisfaction starts creeping in, slowly sinks deeper, and starts affecting their physical and mental health in many ways.

How one perceives oneself is based on one's self-identity. The process of identity development begins in childhood and continues through adolescence into young adulthood. This is a process that is greatly influenced by the messages children receive from the people who are important in their lives. While you as a parent play an important role in your child's life, during their teenage years, their older adolescent or young adult cousins and neighbours become very influential role models.

By watching how older adolescents and young adults behave, and by imitating what the media portrays about them, adolescents learn socially acceptable ways of engaging in intimate relationships.[1] For example, your adolescent child may learn that to be considered 'cool', he/she needs to make a girlfriend/boyfriend. However, what is deemed socially acceptable behaviour need not be desirable, let alone ideal, for the development of children.

'Sexualization' is an umbrella term that is used to describe a variety of social processes that children are exposed to. These include: 1) the attribution of adult sexuality to children, 2) perpetuation of problematically narrow definitions of physical beauty and attractiveness, 3) obsession with weight, shape and size, 4) restrictive definitions of what it means to be male or female, 5) perpetuation of practices that subjugate girls and women, and 6) gender-based violence. The following are three interrelated ways by which the sexualization of children occurs.[2]

The contribution by society

This includes cultural norms, expectations and values that are communicated to children in myriad ways, including through the media. A culture can be infused with sexualized representations of children and young people, suggesting that such sexualization is good and normal. For example, the cosmetics industry has started selling more products specifically to teenagers now. The Associated Chambers of Commerce of India (ASSOCHAM) conducted a nationwide study to look at the consumption of cosmetics and found that 65 per cent of teenagers had reported an increase in spending on branded cosmetics. Both adolescent boys and girls were spending on cosmetics and there was a 75 per cent increase in the amount spent on cosmetics within the past ten years by teenagers. The *Times of India* article that published these findings quoted some adolescent girls saying they used cosmetics, including illuminators, body shimmer, lip gloss, blusher, foundation, and so on, as they had read about the need to start early in order 'to avoid trouble later' and because they could not afford to look less good than their peers.[3] The idea that looking good is in comparison with how others look and that cosmetics enhance looks, as well as the idea that without cosmetics one may have trouble looking attractive, are all ideas manufactured by the cosmetics and advertising industries.

An interpersonal contribution

This includes the expectations of family members, peers, teachers and others the child interacts with, regarding how children should behave. Girls can be treated as, and encouraged to be, sexual objects. For example, some mothers of pre-teens or young teenagers often struggle with the decision regarding whether to allow young girls to get their arms and legs 'waxed'. The idea that body hair is ugly and needs to be removed percolates down from advertisements and a cultural ideal that states that women should not have body hair because it makes them unattractive. At the same time, some families/parents, consciously or otherwise, perpetuate this ideal and allow girls to go for waxing. When waxing becomes the norm, those who do not do so come under pressure to also wax in order to fit in with their peer group.

Self-sexualization

Girls may internalize the sexualizing messages they are exposed to and begin to see themselves as sexual objects. When society, in general, through various forms of media and significant people in a child's life including family and friends, approve of and reward their sexualized behaviour and appearance, girls are likely to internalize these standards and engage in self-sexualization. Hence, when girls insist on buying more revealing clothes or cosmetics or express a dissatisfaction with the shape and size of their bodies, it is because of these messages they have internalized. Similarly, boys who are in middle or high school start visiting the gym to pump heavy weights and use supplements and steroids, which are dangerous for their health.[4, 5] They do so because of the body image-related messages they have internalized.

Parents' Action Plan

The question then is: how do we counter these messages we are bombarded with, some overt ('Fair is beautiful and desirable'), others covert ('Girls should be passive and submissive'). Messages that we, as parents, have internalized and that we communicate in turn ('Boys should be sporty and stay outdoors most of the time' while 'Girls should be dressed prettily'). Messages regarding sex, sexuality, gender-based roles, responsibilities and privilege, as well as gender stereotypes, biases and gender-based violence impact the physical and mental health of our children. Such negative messages not only affect children's safety, well-being and interpersonal relationships, but impact the health of our society and the world as a whole.

It turns out that there is a lot parents can do to counter this. There are three broad areas where we, as parents and concerned adults, can intervene. Firstly, we need to look at the media exposure of our children and make an effort to manage, monitor and modulate media messages. For more information, we can use various resources, such as books and articles on this topic.

Secondly, we need to examine our own values and assumptions, the messages that we have internalized, to critically analyse, challenge and change them. Thirdly, we can begin focusing our energies on the larger cultural and societal messages to raise questions, bring about awareness about biases and stereotypes, and reject societal 'norms' that do not work for us or restrict us and our children.

Manage, Monitor and Modulate Media Exposure

Media education has been shown to help elementary school children evaluate advertising critically and not be influenced by it. It has helped regular viewers of violent programming to reduce aggressive behaviour or question the violence shown. Media education has also helped change the attitudes of youth regarding the intention to drink alcohol.[6] A In fact, one of the studies found that the negative impact of media messages, such as glorifying alcohol use, can be moderated by parental reinforcement or counter-reinforcement of the behaviour shown. The same study, however, noted that the parent's influence on children's behaviour is stronger when children are younger.[7]

The American Academy of Paediatrics,[8] the Media Awareness Network,[9] the Canadian Paediatric Society,[10] among others, have come up with recommendations for parents on how to manage media use in the home, especially with regard to sexual content. These include the following:

Manage

- Start media management and good media habits early, when your child is still young. Doing so is likely to increase your ability to enforce restrictions or influence choices as the child grows older.
- Avoid the use of media as an electronic baby sitter.

- Encourage your child to sample a variety of quality media.
- Limit and focus the time your child spends with media.
- Emphasize alternative activities and ensure that your child's media use is balanced with physical activities, hobbies, creative play and playing outdoors.

Monitor

- Encourage careful selection of programmes to view: Monitor and limit the amount and types of media that your children are accessing.
- Create an 'electronic media-free' environment in your child's room. Keep television, computers, gaming equipment and cellphones with Internet access out of the child's bedroom. This will also ensure that late-night chatting and surfing do not cut into sleep time.
- Preview movies, television programmes, video and computer games as rating systems are not foolproof. Decide for yourself regarding the appropriateness of a programme for your child.

Modulate

- Start with self-regulation. Become a good media role model by selectively using media and limiting your own media choices.
- Take an active role in your child's media exposure. Get involved with the use of media—watch, play and listen with them. Co-view and discuss content with children and adolescents.
- Teach critical viewing skills. Point out to children that everything the media shows is not accurate or factual.
- Talk to your child about stereotypical and violent images in the media and about strategies advertisers use to market

to children. Communicate with your child about sexual health and sexuality as he/she develops, and ensure you discuss any conflicting content that they may have seen in the media. Research indicates that parents 'may be able to reduce the effects of sexual content by watching TV with their teenaged children and discussing their own beliefs about sex and the behaviours portrayed'.[11]

- Pay attention to and openly challenge media messages. Talk with your children about the pressures they see, hear and feel from various media sources to diet and to 'look good'.

Utilize rating systems and guidelines

Learn about the Indian and international rating systems for television, music, movies and video games. These ratings can be helpful in choosing appropriate media for children. For example, the Central Board of Film Certification certifies Indian films under four categories—U: Unrestricted Public Exhibition; UA: Unrestricted Public Exhibition (but with a word of caution that parental discretion is required for children below twelve years); R: Restricted to adults; S: Restricted to any special class of persons.

Television programmes are regulated by the Cable Television Networks Rules, 1994,[12] which underwent revisions and amendments in 2011,[13] delineating the following stringent guidelines regarding the depiction of children and women:

- No programmes should be shown that 'Denigrates women through the depiction in any manner of the figure of a woman, her form or body, or any part thereof in such a way as to have the effect of being indecent, or derogatory to women'. Similarly, no programme should be shown that 'denigrates children'. Instead, cable operators are required to show programmes that 'project women in a positive, leadership role of sobriety, moral and character-building qualities'. Programmes meant for adults should normally be carried in the cable service after 11.00 p.m. and before 6.00 a.m. Care should be taken to ensure that programmes meant for children do not contain any bad language or explicit scenes of violence. Programmes unsuitable for children must not be carried in the cable service at times when the largest number of children are viewing.[14]

- In advertisements, 'Women must not be portrayed in a manner that emphasizes passive, submissive qualities and encourages them to play a subordinate, secondary role in the family and society. The cable operator shall ensure that the portrayal of the female form, in the programmes carried in his cable service is tasteful and aesthetic, and is within the well-established norms of good taste and decency. No advertisement which endangers the safety of children or creates in them any interest in unhealthy practices or shows them begging or in an undignified or indecent manner' are to be shown. 'Indecent, vulgar, suggestive, repulsive or offensive themes or treatment shall be avoided in all advertisements.'[15]

These rules are primarily meant for people who make television programmes and advertisements and can be interpreted in various ways by them. As parents, it is sensible to know the rules so that one knows what one can expect from the films and programmes being broadcast. If, as a parent, you think that the programmes or advertisements being shown do not adhere to these rules, you can raise an objection.

One can also look at some of the international rating systems as a lot of the programming that our children are exposed to are international in origin. Some of these ratings are a bit more detailed and break up the entire age range of two to eighteen years into smaller groups. Watching television or any other form of entertainment media is not recommended for the under-two age group.[16] Programmes are grouped based on guidelines regarding their appropriateness for different age groups and assigned a rating symbol. For example, the following are some of the guidelines used in the film and television classification system in Canada.[17]

Age group two-eight: Programmes for the under-eight age group should not contain any realistic scenes of violence. Any aggressive behaviour shown should be limited and restricted to depictions that are imaginary and unrealistic. Such programmes should contain no nudity, no sexual content at all, and no offensive language. Examples of suitable programmes are *Dora the Explorer*, *Doc McStuffins*, *Wild Kratts* and cartoon films, such as *Cars*.

Age group eight twelve-thirteen: Programmes for this age group should not show that the preferred, acceptable or only way to resolve conflict is through the use of violence. If violence is shown, any realistic depictions should be infrequent, discreet, of low intensity and should also show the consequences of violence. The violence shown must be within the context of the story and may include mild physical violence, comedic violence, comic horror, special effects, fantasy, supernatural or animated violence. These programmes should contain no profanity and no sexual content. Examples of suitable viewing are the cartoon *Transformers* series or the movie *Harry Potter and the Sorcerer's Stone*.

Age group fourteen-eighteen: Programmes for this age group can include controversial themes or issues. Limited and moderate depictions of conflict and/or aggression are acceptable as are physical, fantasy or supernatural violence. Also allowed are infrequent and mild profanity, mildly suggestive language and brief scenes of nudity as well as limited and discreet sexual references or content when appropriate to the storyline or theme. (Some of these programmes may also be viewed by the eight–fourteen years age group, but only after parents preview the programme and think it is appropriate; they should also view the programme/movie with their child.) Films like *Amazing Spiderman 2* or *PK* can be shown. Some of the programmes and films for this age group may, however, not be appropriate for a younger audience at all and should not be viewed by younger children. Such programmes and movies include intense scenes of violence, strong or frequent use of profanity, scenes of nudity and/or sexual activity within the context of the story.

Age group eighteen and over: Programmes for this age group include depictions of violence which, while integral to the development of plot, character or themes, are intended for adult viewing only. These programmes and movies are not suitable for children under eighteen years of age. Such programmes may also contain graphic language and explicit portrayals of sex and/or nudity. For example, serials like *Game of Thrones*.

Knowledge of the various rating symbols is useful as it can guide you in choosing age-appropriate films or programmes for your children. In addition, as a parent, you can use the above rating guidelines or any of the other standard age-based rating guidelines from any country to independently decide on the appropriateness of films, cartoons and programmes for children. There are also organizations with a web presence that provide reviews and parent-based ratings.[18] This would mean that regardless of a rating symbol, such as U, UA or R, being present or not, you do need to preview or do enough research on the content of any programme that you intend to allow your child to watch.

It is important to remember, though, that any cartoon series that shows the same set of characters who relate with each other in the same way or are engaged in similar behaviour in each episode, such as in the *Doraemon* series, exerts a great influence on the child's development. Such repeated viewing of the same set of behaviours results in children learning those behaviours and imitating them. It also teaches them to conduct relationships or resolve any conflict in the ways shown in the programmes. If it is a cartoon series, such as *Doc McStuffins*, the child may learn some positive ideas/behaviours. This is because the *Doc McStuffins* series shows a young African-American girl who is very influenced by her mother who is a doctor. Her father is the homemaker and the parents work as a team in bringing up their daughter. In this way, the series presents positive role models and non-stereotyped gender roles. However, if it is a series such as *Doraemon*, the impact may not be so desirable. Most of the *Doraemon* episodes show the main character Nobita getting into trouble, crying and complaining, and Gian, the big bully, beating people up. Nobita's female friend Shizuka is always demure and passive. These are not behaviours most parents want their children to expect or accept as normal, or to imitate in any way.

In the end, it is about making sound choices. There are non-stereotyped, non-sexualized, educational and entertainment media options available. It is just a question of doing enough research to find the right sources of education and entertainment for your child. Anita Sarkeesian, media critic and gamer, runs a video web series that looks critically at the representation of women in media. She is currently running a series on positive female characters in video games and has recommended 'Jade—Beyond Good and Evil', a video game for children, for its relatively non-violent and healthy portrayal of a female character in video games.[19] There are also 'social impact games' that have been created to promote 'humanitarian and educational efforts'.[20] Hence, cartoons, films and video games can have a beneficial and educational impact on children, but a parent needs to do the homework and then choose wisely.

Challenge and Change Internalized Attitudes and Communicate Healthy Attitudes to Children

Change your own attitudes and behaviours regarding shape and size: Focus on building a healthy lifestyle and supportive relationships. Dr Paula Levine has come up with some suggestions regarding dieting, the drive for thinness and body dissatisfaction.[21] She suggests that parents should examine their own 'attitudes, beliefs, prejudices, and behaviours about food, weight, body image, physical appearance, health, and exercise'. Men should also 'examine their own "weightist" attitudes and behaviour toward females'.

As parents are role models, it is important to begin by adopting a healthy lifestyle and a realistic mindset towards size and shape. Parents, especially mothers, who are constantly dieting or complaining about their weight send a negative signal to children about food and weight. Extremes in terms of eating or exercising are healthy neither for parents nor for children.

Focusing too much on one's appearance and complaining about not being able to wear certain clothes or engage in certain activities because of one's weight or shape also sends a signal to children that appearance is more important than other qualities. Move away from a negative focus on appearance—relax, accept and enjoy your own body shape and size and appreciate all the different shapes and sizes that you see around you. This also means accepting the shape and size of your child and letting him/her know shape and size does not matter.

Adopt exercising habits that are sustainable and enjoyable. As a family, make it a point to enjoy the outdoors—you can play games or take up any other outdoor activities. Adopt healthy eating habits, eat nutritious food, and make a variety of food available in the house. In terms of parenting, do not use food as a reward or punishment.

Unless advised by a medical professional for a specific medical reason, do not limit your child's food either. Encourage your children's natural tendency to eat in response to hunger and let them develop their own sense about when they are full by allowing them to decide how much they want to eat. Most of all, do not prevent children from eating anything saying it will make them 'fat'.

The most important thing to remember is that 'thin' is not necessarily healthy. The media has tended to exaggerate the dangers of being anything but thin. Research on children of different weights has shown that 'only children who were obese at thirteen showed an increased risk of obesity as adults. No excess adult health risk from childhood or teenage overweight was found. Being thin in childhood offered no protection against adult fatness, and the thinnest children tended to have the highest adult risk at every level of adult obesity'.[22] Hence, being thin in childhood has no connection with being healthy in adulthood, and being overweight in childhood or during the teenage years does not leave one more prone to health issues in adulthood.

Focus, instead, on building healthy, supportive relationships. 'Teach children about good relationships and how to deal with difficulties when they arise. Males and females alike may use food to express or numb themselves instead of dealing with difficult feelings or relationships. Because of messages that suggest that the perfect body will dissolve all relationship problems, young people often put energy into changing their bodies instead of their feelings or their relationships.'[23]

It is essential to build your children's self-esteem and celebrate their unique qualities. In terms of your own attitudes towards your children, it is important to set aside the media definition of beauty or attractiveness. Recognize and celebrate your child's qualities, whatever they may be, beginning at birth onwards. Each child is unique, with individualistic qualities.

As children reach adolescence, it is doubly important to focus on the positive aspects of their personality, talents and abilities—their ability to stand up for themselves, to relate well with others, the calmness of their temperament, their inquisitiveness, their physical strength and agility, and so on. It is also important to encourage children to equate their personal worth with the positive aspects of their personality and not with their external appearance. This is a time when children are under a great amount of pressure from the media and society, including peers, to conform to prevailing definitions of physical appearance and behaviour, including experimenting with sex, alcohol and drugs.

Adolescence is the time when children need the support of both their parents to resist social pressures and take healthy decisions. It is important to talk openly with children about the pressures they may be going through and encourage their efforts to not give in to the pressures they face. It is important that fathers remain close to and be supportive of their daughters as they experiment and struggle with their body image, grooming and cosmetic issues, flirtatiousness and sexuality.[24]

As children grow older, discuss with them the dangers of excessive dieting and exercising and the myth that a specific shape or size will automatically lead to happiness and success. Encourage children to be physically active and engage in sports of their choice. Help children accept and enjoy their bodies and encourage physical activity for the joy of being active, not with the aim of losing weight. Research has found that during adolescence, boys are equally divided between wanting to lose weight and increasing weight. Research also shows that body dissatisfaction in males is associated with poor psychological adjustment, eating disorders, steroid use, exercise dependence and other health issues.[25]

Of significance are the findings from a study conducted across twenty-four countries, which suggests that enhanced parent communication might contribute to less body dissatisfaction in girls. Also, better communication with the father can help avoid body weight dissatisfaction in boys.[26] Hence, communication between parents, both mother and father, and children is really the key to preventing body weight and shape dissatisfaction in boys and girls.

Children learn to communicate when they know they will be listened to and that their thoughts and ideas will be valued by you as a parent. Communication is a two-way street and it is as important to truly listen to what children and teenagers are saying as is sharing with them what one thinks and feels. In general, communication with parents also helps children to build confidence, knowing their thoughts and feelings are respected, and this adds to their self-esteem in a significant way.

Encourage critical thinking: Empower through information

Dr Michael Levine and Dr Linda Smolak believe that the 'only sure antidote to the tendency to conform to the powerful seduction of the media and peer pressure is the ability to think critically. Parents have to encourage critical thinking early, and educators have to continue the mission'. Critical thinking means teaching children 'how to think, not what to think, and to encourage them to disagree, challenge, brainstorm alternatives'. They stress on the fact that 'Girls especially need to learn that men are not the ultimate authorities and that they themselves have something important to contribute'.[27] Critical thinking requires that we give our children accurate, factual information so that they can weigh all sides of an argument.

Encouraging critical thinking also implies talking to children about sex and sexuality in a factual, age-appropriate manner. Talking about sex and sexuality is not a one-time conversation, so keep looking for opportunities. These may come in the form of questions children ask or events that they encounter. The songs they hear and the programmes and films they watch may also provide the context for having these conversations.

It is important to counter what the media shows in terms of sex and sexuality and the myths and misperceptions it creates. Some of the myths that have been identified are: Most young people and most adults have sex on a regular basis; sex often occurs between people who barely know each other; sex has no context or consequences; sex just happens and people have no control over their impulses and desires; infidelity or sex with multiple partners is common; and so on.

Communicate your own values about sex—whether premarital sex is acceptable or not, the importance of being in a committed and mutually respectful relationship, the fact that sex is only one aspect of a committed relationship, learning to communicate effectively, and learning to say 'no' when uncomfortable or feeling pressurized in a relationship. As fathers and mothers, make it a point to talk to your sons about the way body shape and sexuality (for both boys and girls) are manipulated by the media, and the struggle their sisters or female friends have in trying to conform or not to conform to those images.[28]

Intervene when required

It is also important to look out for the warning signs of eating disorders—anorexia and bulimia. Some of these behaviours can appear before puberty and include refusing typical family meals, skipping meals, making negative statements about oneself and others, such as 'I'm too fat' or 'She's too fat', being too critical of how one looks in different clothes and finding it difficult to choose what to wear, withdrawal from friends, irritability and depression, signs of extreme dieting, bingeing or purging.[29]

One of the well-known people to have suffered from bulimia was Princess Diana, the ex-wife of Britain's Prince Charles. Princess Diana admitted that she began to follow a strict diet after people made comments on TV and in magazines about her 'pudgy' appearance. Once she started dieting, she couldn't stop.[30]

Studies have also found the symptoms of anorexia[31] and bulimia in Indian teenagers. One of the studies noted that there is a higher prevalence of bulimia-type symptoms as compared to anorexia, and while the prevalence is lower than in Western countries, it is similar to other non-Western cultures.[32] Indian children with eating disorders tend to show a 'higher drive for thinness and body dissatisfaction, external pressures, mood susceptibility of feeding patterns, perfectionism, occurrence of negative life events and presence and adequacy of emotional support system'.[33]

If you notice your child showing any bulimic or anorexic behaviour on a consistent basis or suspect that your child may have an eating disorder, get him or her help. Consult a medical as well as a mental health professional who can help treat different aspects of this disorder. When seeking a consultation, make sure to ask about the professionals' credentials, their level of training and experience in working with children and teenagers on these issues.

When it comes to sexual activity, 'As always, open communication during childhood and through adolescence will help you define and augment the information your daughter has already received from watching you and from listening to myriad other voices. Providing an accepting environment at home will further enable her to feel comfortable discussing sensitive topics with you. Starting with pubescence, girls tend to turn more to their mothers than to their fathers. A single father should support his daughter in finding women such as an aunt, teacher, or coach who can provide her with the female role that can help in developing identity. But fathers should remain involved. Without a father's continuing interest in her, many teen girls start seeking inappropriate male attention outside the house. Research shows that teens who feel connected to their family and school are less likely to initiate premature sexual activity'.[34]

But if you do find out that your son or daughter has a 'boyfriend' or 'girlfriend' and you suspect they may already be sexually active, the most important thing to do is to not overreact. Gone are the days when you could lock up your 'Juliet' and banish the 'Romeo'. In fact, these tactics often fail because it gives young people further incentive to find other ways to meet their 'Romeo' or 'Juliet' and to make greater efforts to hide their activities from you. It is very natural, if one looks at it from a developmental perspective, that adding a dash of dare and excitement to a teenager's relationship will make it more interesting and enticing. Hence, locking up or banning is not an option. At the same time, beating around the bush is also not an effective tactic.

The best approach to take is to ask your child about his/her sexual activity. Share what your concerns may be about early sexual activity. Talk about pregnancy and sexually transmitted diseases. Talk about the fact that many young people, who engaged in sex early, later expressed regret at having done so. Explain that sex is one aspect of a respectful, committed relationship, and it takes years to build such a relationship. Ask your child to wait until he/she is sure this is the relationship he/she wants to be in for a long time. Some experts from this field point out that the 'abstinence-only' sex education programmes in the US have had a lack of success due to the media focus on 'non-abstinence'.[35]

Rather than blaming individuals, that is, your child, the boyfriend or girlfriend, anybody's family and so on—look at the larger socio-cultural influences and think of how you can address these. A very influential group of people is your child's group of friends. Research has found that children who are in their early teenage years tend to challenge the experience and authority of their parents more than younger children or older teenagers. These early teenagers tend to listen to their friends whose opinions they value more. Older teenagers, on the other hand, are equally influenced by their friends as well as by adults.[36] This means that as a parent you need to be aware of who your child's friends are, especially when they enter their teenage years and onwards. In fact, you can intervene at the larger friend circle level. You can talk to your child's school authorities and see if they can talk to this age group about sex and sexuality, and encourage critical thinking on media influences. If not, perhaps you can try to do so yourself.

As parents and concerned adults, you can also involve yourself in campaigns that challenge some of the stereotypes and biases we and our children are faced with. 'Women of Worth', a movement organized to empower women, took out a campaign to challenge the perpetuation of the Indian bias towards fair skin through prominent advertisements of fairness products.[37]

The Advertising Council of India in 2014 finally took up the issue and expressed its concern regarding the same and asked companies not to perpetuate the 'fair skin is good', 'dark skin is bad' bias through advertisements.[38] While this is a positive step, it will not stop companies from producing and selling fairness products altogether. Sale of such products will cease only when we, as consumers, stop buying fairness products and matrimonial advertisements stop talking about 'fairness' as a desirable quality in a spouse. Ultimately, as Mahatma Gandhi famously said, 'Be the change you want to see in the world.'

Chapter 8

INVESTING IN A FUTURE FREE OF SEXUAL VIOLENCE

*'You may never know what results come of your action,
but if you do nothing there will be no result.'*
—Mahatma Gandhi

Sexual violence, a form of gender-based violence, is a reality in today's world. Open the newspaper from any part of the world and you will find incidents of sexual violence. No place in the world—the developed world, developing world, urban or rural areas—is free of this type of violence. While girls and young women face sexual violence more often, boys and young men can also become its victims.

There are different ways in which children and young people face sexual or gender-based exploitation and violence:

- Child sexual abuse, incest or rape
- Stalking and sexual harassment of girls and young women in public spaces
- Ostracization, harassment or bullying by the peer group of girls or boys who challenge gender stereotypes or behave in ways that are contrary to the expectations for their gender
- Ostracization, harassment, bullying of and discrimination against young people who are homosexual, bisexual or transgender
- Sex trafficking, pornography and prostitution
- Sexualization

Except for sexualization, the other types of sexual violence mentioned above are quite overt and self-explanatory. They have also been discussed in the previous chapters of this book. However, sexualization is a process that needs to be examined carefully and understood for it has far-reaching ramifications for the psychological and physical health and safety of girls and women. Sexualization is a complex and often covert process that both perpetuates and is perpetuated by sexual exploitation and violence.

The American Psychological Association (APA)[1] explains that sexualization occurs when any of the following occur:

A person's value comes only from his or her sexual appeal or behaviour, to the exclusion of other characteristics: There are many examples of this aspect, especially as portrayed by celebrities. Scholars have pointed out that celebrities have often used sex as a 'metamorphosis'. They have studied how younger female musicians, such as Christina Aguilera, Faith Hill and Britney Spears, have used their sexuality to appear more mature and 'edgier' when they wanted to be perceived as 'adult musicians' and not just teen pop stars. For example, Britney Spears presented her 'mature' image at the 2001 MTV Awards by appearing in a nude body stocking.

Attention-grabbing actions such as these often lead to the media and fans focusing on the person's body and sexuality rather than their talent and the quality of their work. Such actions also communicate to impressionable teenagers and young people that the way to catch attention and be perceived as 'mature and successful' in a certain industry or area of work is by using one's body and sexuality and being a 'sexual object'.[2]

A person feels impelled to meet high standards that equate physical attractiveness (narrowly defined) with being sexy: The definition of who is physically attractive has shrunk to weight and 'curves' as the only criteria for being 'sexy', which is further broken up into micro-measurements. The Indian media imposes an extremely strict standard for appearance, and criticism abounds if a Bollywood actress does not meet some unachievable ideal of 'sexy'.

With eye-catching titles, such as '10 Bikini-Clad Bollywood Actresses Who Were an Eyesore!' the media makes statements such as 'Bollywood hotties happily shed their clothes to show off their bikini bods, but does donning that two-piece really make them look sexy? Nah, not always! Being too skinny for the bikini or too fat for it, these actresses really need a reality check on how bad they looked wearing the two-piece.'[3] The implication of statements such as these are that clothes, especially those that reveal more of the body, are related to being 'sexy'. In addition, there is a very specific physical criterion for being considered 'sexy'. Anyone who does not meet the implied criteria or does not wear clothes supposed to be 'sexy' is not attractive.

A person is sexually objectified—that is, made into a thing for others' sexual use, rather than seen as a person with the capacity for independent action and decision-making: A study commissioned by the UN and the Geena Davis foundation that looked at how women are represented in films worldwide found that Indian films were among the worst in terms of featuring fewer female characters with speaking roles (24.9 per cent) as compared to male characters. In addition, women characters who were shown as earning a living through formal work in the films reviewed formed only 22.5 per cent, while male working characters were 77.5 per cent. 'Across notable professions, male characters outnumbered their female counterparts as attorneys and judges (13 to 1), professors (16 to 1), medical practitioners (5 to 1), and in STEM fields (7 to 1).'[4]

The study further reported that 'Sexualization is the standard for female characters globally: girls and women are twice as likely as boys and men to be shown in sexually revealing clothing, partially or fully naked, thin, and five times as likely to be referenced as attractive. Teen females (13–20 years old) are just as likely as young adult females (21–39 years old) to be sexualized'.

Hence, women and girls, even in fiction, are not treated as equal to men. This further perpetuates the idea that women are 'eye candies' and not individuals with the ability to think and act. They are not considered as people who can play a significant, active role in society or have the ability to impact society.

Sexuality is inappropriately imposed upon a person: While any person, whether male or female, of any age can be sexualized, 'when children are imbued with adult sexuality, it is often imposed upon them rather than chosen by them'. The APA further clarifies that 'self-motivated sexual exploration' or 'age-appropriate exposure to information about sexuality' is not sexualization. What this means is that exposing a six-year-old to sexual information that is meant for a sixteen-year-old is inappropriate and potentially harmful for the six-year-old but not for the sixteen-year-old.

Sexualization has far-reaching consequences as 'what young women believe about themselves and how they feel in the present moment were shaped by how they were treated and what they were exposed to when they were girls'. Hence, sexualization as a process begins exerting its influence when children are very young. By the time adulthood is attained, sexualizing messages have been internalized and further sexualization is accepted as normal.

In addition, both boys and girls are exposed to the same

messages, which means that boys then learn to view girls and women as sexualized objects. Unless boys see girls as equals, they are unlikely to respect them.[5] These attitudes are often carried forward into adulthood.

Sexual violence and its impact

Media, in general, reflects prevalent societal norms and often reinforces them. This overarching societal lack of respect for girls and women is reflected in, and reinforced by, the media in overt and covert ways. Studies have looked at various forms of the media and the disturbing tolerance and perpetuation of sexual violence couched in terms such as 'harmless' entertainment.

A study examined sexual remarks made on prime time comedies on American television and found that 23 per cent of the comments reflected sexual behaviours that were forms of sexual harassment, including leering, ogling, staring and catcalling at female characters. Additionally, 16.5 per cent of the sexual remarks made were about women's body parts or nudity. A majority of these comments (85 per cent) came from men. Overall, 78 per cent of the sexual harassment on prime time television was focused on using demeaning terms for women or sexualization of their bodies.

Similarly, an analysis of workplace-based situation comedies also turned up an average of 3.3 per cent of gender harassment (defined as jokes, looks, calls) and 0.5 per cent of sexual harassment (touching, asking for 'favours', persistent unwanted invites for dates) per episode, while 74 per cent of the episodes contained at least one episode of gender harassment in the form of jokes, most accompanied by laughter tracks.[6] The most worrying aspect of such programmes is that they normalize sexual harassment and violence.

Sexual violence has far-reaching consequences. It not only impacts the victim but greatly affects his/her interpersonal relationships and society, in general. Child sexual abuse, incest and rape deeply harm the physical, mental and social well-being of the victim. Victims of sexual violence often struggle with negative effects well into adulthood. Many go through depression, anxiety disorders, poor self-esteem, suicide attempts, eating disorders, drug/alcohol abuse, post-traumatic stress disorder, dissociation, sexual difficulties, self-harming behaviours and may develop personality disorders. Some victims, especially male victims, may show aggressive behaviour and commit crimes as juveniles and adults.[7]

Sexualized harassment is behaviour that a person or group of people are subjected to due to their gender or sexual orientation. The behaviours that form sexualized harassment have been listed as 'verbal name-calling, labelling ('slut', 'fag'), spreading rumours about someone, groping or commenting on someone's body, sexuality or gender expression, commenting about someone's body type, physical/ emotional/verbal acts of violence based on a label (for example, 'slut-shaming'), physical/ emotional/verbal acts of violence based on sexuality/gender expression or gender, creating or facilitating an environment that is perceived as violent by someone through enforcing ideas about gender, physical control of public spaces and excluding bodies based on gender or sexuality, sharing images/stories of people without consent about their personal sexual choices, bodies, sexuality or gender, street/public space sexualized harassment through name-calling or soliciting sexualized attention.

Sexualized harassment not only impacts a person/group's emotional well-being; it also impinges on personal boundaries and physical choices. It is believed that around 80 per cent of women and most Lesbian, Gay, Bisexual, Transgender, and Queer (LGBTQ) people around the world have experienced street or public space sexualized harassment.[8]

Overall, sexualization, even in its 'milder' forms, has been found to negatively affect cognitive performance in college-aged women. As Carolyn Heldman so eloquently explains in her 'The Sexy Lie' talk for TEDxYouth, SanDiego, that if you are so caught up in worrying about how you look and with comparing your appearance with others, you do not have the mental space to focus on other problems. Research has shown that *just* being exposed to sexualized media images on a consistent basis also contributes to body dissatisfaction, eating disorders, low self-esteem, feeling depressed and physical health problems in high-school-aged girls.[9]

Taking steps to bring about equality

Sexual violence or gender-based violence is rooted in the sex-based, age-old dichotomy of roles, responsibilities, power and privilege. It is not an equal division, since men have been favoured with greater power and presence in the public sphere. In addition, it is a rigid division that does not allow for many changes.

There are many examples of this dichotomy. One somewhat simplified example is that women have traditionally been sanctioned the responsibility and privilege of rearing children, but men have not. Moreover, housework and child-rearing are still undervalued. Men who want to stay home and bring up children to the exclusion of other roles are often viewed as aberrations. Instead, men have been accorded the responsibility to earn and financially support their families, along with the power to make social and financial decisions for the family. Women who only want to take on work outside the home and not take care of any household or child-rearing responsibilities are also viewed as aberrations.

In addition, certain characteristics are attributed to women, such as being emotionally expressive, nurturing, collaborative and non-confrontational. On the other hand, certain personality characteristics are seen as 'male characteristics', such as being aggressive, assertive, independent, controlled and emotionally non-expressive, except for expressing negative emotions such as anger. Female characteristics are seen as well suited for the private sphere, while male characteristics are seen as adapted for the public sphere.

Due to the rigidly assigned roles, often both men and women are not able to fully realize their potential, and feel unhappy, stuck as they are with these roles. Despite all the technological advances, the age-old stereotypical notion prevails that women are naturally adapted to rearing children and managing family relationships but are not equipped to run corporations and to be strong leaders. Men, on the other hand, are also considered as unsuited to leading a purely domestic life. They have to portray qualities supposed to be masculine, whether they can and want to, or not. Remarks, such as 'Don't cry like a girl', 'Stop being a sissy', 'She's a tomboy', are all remarks that are often thoughtlessly made, but which ensure that gender messages are passed on and internalized, maintaining the status quo.

Biologically, boys and girls have an equal capacity to experience and express a range of emotions. The limitations we create are artificial. Each child is born with a certain temperament, but these temperamental characteristics are not based on gender—some boys can be more gentle and nurturing than some girls, and some girls can be more energetic and fearless than some boys. Children should be able to seek out experiences and grow up to live the life they choose based on their interests and temperament, rather than dictated by gender definitions created by society. Gender-based violence will stop only when there is true equality[10] and gender ceases to matter.

The American Association of University Women (AAUW) points out that: 'Many of the biographies of the best-known innovators of our time are filled with childhoods of taking things apart and putting them back together. And too few of these famous innovators are women'. They encourage parents to let 'the girls in your life get dirty. Let them wear out the knees in their clothes and get dirt under their nails. Let them take apart their toys and find out how they work. Don't let your concern about their politeness or cleanliness get in the way of their delight in exploring the world around them. And don't let your fear of seeing them fail stop them from finding their own solutions'.

The recommendation then is to drastically reduce an emphasis on appearance and, instead, let girls explore and experience more meaningful aspects of life. Encouraging girls to be 'doers', and not passive participants or followers is vital. 'Girls who are given the freedom to explore and discover things for themselves are more likely to grow into women who confidently explore fields like engineering and technology—where women are sorely needed.'[11] To bring about equality, more women need to come out into the public sphere and take up roles of power and responsibility.

Men Against Violence and Abuse (MAVA), an Indian organization working on increasing awareness and preventing gender-based violence, believes that 'only when men break the moulds of society and express rather than suppress their emotions, they can become less violent towards women'.[12] Such organizations not only create awareness about gender-based violence and its negative impact on both men and women, they also encourage healthy relationships and attitudes that consider equality of the two genders is essential. In addition, such programmes also create space and acceptance for men and women who do not follow strict traditional gender roles. For example, they help create acceptance for boys who are more sensitive and emotionally expressive and girls who are more active and assertive.

The UN has come up with a gender-based violence prevention programme for young people ranging in age from five to twenty-five years. Their belief is that prevention is better than intervention alone, and prevention is best achieved by involving young people. Although many programmes provide support services to victims of gender-based violence, more are needed. In addition, Indian laws are quite strong and efforts are on to implement them better. However, laws and intervention/support services become applicable after acts of gender violence have been committed. The idea is to not get stuck with creating more band aids for wounds, but to prevent wounds from being inflicted altogether.

While legal consequences are meant to act as deterrents, a change in attitudes is likely to result in a more sustainable and long-lasting impact on gender equality. The UN says that discussing gender and violence in an age-appropriate manner with young people will lead to a change in attitudes and perceptions of young people, which can lead to a long-term change in behaviour.

Steps parents can take

Some people may view equality as a utopian concept and express their doubt that equality between the two genders can be achieved. We can attain this goal only if we try hard. As adults, we carry the responsibility and the ability to initiate change. But this change has to first come from within.

Adopt a belief in equality by a change in attitude

As parents, we can try changing our attitudes by first examining our own internalized gender definitions and challenge them. Children learn the most from their parents. Our words speak to them, but our actions and behaviour often speak louder. In our minds, we have to start seeing our children as the individuals they are, devoid of the boy/girl label. This also means that we have to become more conscious and aware as parents.

Introspect and change your gender attitudes

It is important to look at your own upbringing and ideas about men and women. Often, the template for ideas about men and women is formed in childhood based on the relationships one observes, most significantly the relationship between one's parents.

Many men have talked about growing up in a household where their father was as involved in the household tasks as their mother. Or growing up in a family environment where they were entrusted with various household chores by their mother, including helping out in the kitchen. Growing up in such environments has helped these men appreciate the contribution of women, and also learn not to segregate tasks as either a man's or a woman's task, which, in turn, helps in acquiring a respect for women and their contribution to their families and society.[13]

Except for giving birth and nursing a baby, there are no specific tasks that only men or women can do. There may be some men who are physically stronger than women but there are also some women who are physically stronger and more agile than some men. Hence, when it comes to tasks, everyone can learn to do everything.

Stretch your own gender boundaries by getting involved in tasks that are supposed to be undertaken only by the opposite gender. Children often learn that they can do any type of work by watching their parents engage with different tasks. If your sons and daughters see you do a variety of tasks, regardless of gender, they will see it as normal, acceptable and doable. If, as a man, you have not already done so, then it is important to start taking women and girls 'more seriously for what they say, feel and do, and focus less on the way they look.[14]

Implement the concept of equality with your children

As parents, an important gift we can give to our children is to refrain from fitting them into a box or force a definition on them about who they 'should' be. Examine and challenge everything, from the labels you use, such as 'sissy' and 'tomboy', to the classes you send your children to, such as sending girls to dance classes and boys to soccer coaching. Why can it not be the other way round? If we ask for and insist on soccer coaching for girls and dance classes for boys, we will get them.

Ask your sons to help out in the kitchen, keeping in mind that learning to cook is a basic life skill which is as important for boys as it is for girls. Discuss your interests, even if it is cricket and cars, with both your sons and daughters. Equality means being open to and helping both our sons and daughters regardless of their gender.

Understand the temperament of each child; if your son is emotional and sensitive and your daughter energetic and assertive, provide opportunities for them accordingly, to achieve their potential. We will truly achieve equality when we are able to help fulfil a son's dream of becoming a classical dancer or support his choice to stay at home to raise children, and equally support a daughter's choice to become an entrepreneur or a deep sea diver!

Equality is important as it brings a sense of respect for the other and also makes unequal behaviour unacceptable.[15] Violence and exploitation cannot exist or be supported in an environment of equality.

Challenge sexualization

We are, and have been, exposed to sexualizing influences as much as our children currently are. From the messages we received from our families to the socio-cultural expectations around us, we have internalized many of these messages.

Become conscious consumers

Parents may erroneously believe that the media affects everyone else but not them and their families.[16] The fact is that none of us is impervious to the influence of the media. As part of a very interesting TedxJaffa Talk on Pornography, Ran Gavrieli, who is involved in gender studies at the Tel Aviv University, shared that he stopped watching porn as it brought a lot of anger and violence into his sexual fantasies, anger and violence which had not existed before he started watching pornography. He also realized that by watching porn, he was supporting the 'filmed prostitution' industry, which exists due to the sexual exploitation of girls and women.

Many of us have probably gone through the same experience. Consciously or unconsciously, we do take in messages and imitate behaviour due to our exposure to different forms of media. It is important to become more aware as parents so we can help our children to be discerning about the content of sexualizing messages they get from the media.

In addition, it is important to take a stand and not support pornography or other 'institutions' that cast women as objects for the pleasure of men, objects without personal integrity.[17]

Help children become media aware

Talk, talk, and then, talk some more. Have open discussions with children and young people about the images of men and women they are exposed to in the media. Take a stand on the books, stories and movies young children are exposed to.

If you don't bring fairy tale movies/books into the house, it is possible your children may see them at a friend's house. Discuss with your sons and daughters what you think about such books or stories. For example, do they perpetuate negative stereotypes? Why should the fairy tale princess have to be so pretty or thin or fair? Or why does she need to be rescued by a prince? Why can't she solve her problems herself? Or why is a Barbie doll's figure so thin? Are real people like her? And so on.

As children grow older, you can discuss the images or stories they are exposed to through films and music videos. Challenge any stereotypes there. Children may protest and young people may disagree when you have such a discussion, but your words are certain to have a more long-term impact. Remember, parents are more influential than they realize.

Break the cycle of violence

The cycle of violence is often transmitted from one generation to the other. 'Male children who witness violence have an increased risk of becoming abusive later in life if there is no appropriate intervention. Likewise, female children who witness violence or are abused may be at risk of being further abused in adulthood if appropriate interventions are not made available.'[18]

Get help for yourself if you have been a victim

As a parent, you are the biggest role model your child has. Global statistics seem to indicate that one in three women may have been a victim of gender violence at some time in their lives.[19] Hence, if you are in an abusive or violent relationship, the most important step you can take for your child is to end the violence. This may mean asserting yourself in the relationship or finding ways to deal with issues in a non-violent manner with your partner, or ending the relationship if the violence does not end. If you have been a victim of sexual violence in the past and are suffering from the long-term impact of such abuse, it is imperative to seek help and to heal.

The reason for taking these actions is simple—as long as you are suffering and preoccupied with your own issues, you will not be completely available to your child. In addition, through your actions of either ending a violent relationship, changing your own behaviour and finding non-violent ways to dealing with interpersonal conflict, or taking steps to recover, heal and find a path to growth after suffering violence, you become a role model for your child. Boys and girls learn to neither perpetuate nor accept violence.

Make your home a 'No violence' zone

It is important to practise what you preach. Treating all members of the family with respect, regardless of gender or age, sets up an example for children. Fathers, as significant male role models, play a particularly important role through demonstrating respectful and non-violent behaviour: 'Model patience, compassion, tenderness, fallibility, and most importantly, the capacity and desire to listen'.[20]

Differences exist wherever human beings exist, and yes, you will quarrel and have heated arguments. But it is crucial to resolve interpersonal differences in a non-violent manner. As parents, remember that how you conduct your 'fights' predicts how your children are likely to behave when they fight in their own relationships.

Taking a clear stand against any violence in the house teaches children that it is not okay. They may not always be able to show very mature conduct in their interactions with each other, but they will get the message loud and clear. As they grow up, they will also be able to integrate it in their behaviour. Equally importantly, they will expect non-violent behaviour from others and will not tolerate violence in relationships.

Speak up against sexualizing attitudes and violence in your community.

As Kate Gilmore of UN's population fund states, 'The thing that flourishes violence is silence. If you haven't declared you are against violence against women, you are a part of it. There is nowhere to hide.'[21] Take a stand against violence and make your stance known.

The most significant legacy we can leave for our children is a world that is more peaceful and egalitarian. And the change begins with us, with our immediate environment. It is a given that with exposure to an extremely networked world, we are also exposed to sexualizing attitudes in varied and numerous ways. But even if we change what is closer to us, our immediate environment, we can create an impact.

We can start challenging gender-biased attitudes in social spaces and workplaces. Support women colleagues and neighbours as they strive for equality in different ways. 'Work toward and speak out for women's rights: to fair pay, to safety, to respect, and to control of their bodies.'[22] Speak up and speak out against sexual violence.

Create awareness by getting involved with organizations working in this area. Take action by boycotting or opposing advertisements, songs, television programmes and movies that sexualize women and girls. There are many actions we can take and many ways we can be involved. Get active!

CONCLUSION: MORAL OF THE STORY

In India, sex and sexuality continue to be thorny topics. When it comes to children and sexuality, most adults pretend they do not exist. However, sexuality is an integral part of the human experience and develops from infancy onwards. While schools and parents often don't want to broach this topic, everyone else in the child's environment appears to be talking about it incessantly. Advertisements, films, music, video games, books, magazines and the ever-present Internet bombard our children with countless sexualizing messages: 'Thin is good,' 'Fair is lovely,' 'Expose skin to be considered desirable,' 'Having sex is the "in" thing,' 'Sex has nothing to do with commitment.' 'Anything less than "perfect" looks is "ordinary"', which implies 'unattractive', 'ugly', 'unworthy'. These messages minimize the importance of inner qualities, temperament and abilities.

Our children are growing up and developing their sense of self in a hyper-sexualized environment, whether we like it or not. Most importantly, they are also developing their sexual identity and a sense of their own sexuality, whether we help them in this process or not. The developing sexuality of children is influenced by their family's values, friends' attitudes and socio-cultural messages that they receive via their exposure to various forms of media. Hence, as a parent, you may be only one of multiple sources of information and influence for your child. However, you are the most important and influential source and can reduce the negative impact of the other sources.

There are many ways by which a parent's morals, values and attitudes towards sexuality get communicated to children. From a young age, children form perceptions related to their body based on our reactions to their exploration and expression of sexuality. Our comfort or discomfort with our own sexuality also gets conveyed to children by the way we conduct our intimate relationships. Often, the parents' marital relationship—the way emotions are expressed or conflict is resolved by the parents, or the way roles and responsibilities are divided in the family—provides a template for the child. You may have noticed that you or your spouse/partner often behave, consciously or unconsciously, the way your parents behaved with each other. Similar may be the fate of your children.

This does not mean that your child's adult relationships or romantic partners will necessarily be a replica of yours, but their expectations from their relationships may be based on what they have seen and experienced in childhood. Whether your child will expect to be an equal partner in his/her marriage or will accept a more traditional division of roles and responsibilities is likely to be based on what he/she witnesses at home now. Sunita is a thirty-five-year-old woman who is aiming to separate from her violent husband who beats her and the children. Her own father was a soft-spoken person and she had never witnessed domestic violence or been beaten up as a child. She has been working for a few years now and just about manages to support herself and her children financially. However, Sunita is very clear that though life may not be easy as a single parent, she will no longer tolerate her husband's violence. It is mainly her experience of growing up with safety and dignity which is helping her find the strength to reject domestic violence now.

Coming back to our role as parents, while, as a parent, you may want to protect your child from all negative experiences, including the bully in the park, the fact is that you cannot be omnipresent. While we cannot create a protective bubble around

Conclusion: Moral of the Story

our children, we can help them build a strong foundation to deal with the instabilities of life. The building blocks of this foundation are positive self-esteem, a comfortable and positive relationship with one's body, comfort with expressing one's sexual needs and desires, and the ability to seek and maintain healthy, respectful and supportive relationships. The good news for parents is that we all have the ability and special privilege of being able to provide the magic ingredient that goes into these building blocks. And the magic ingredient is our relationship with our child. More specifically still, the one ingredient that has been found to be the most influential is communication between parents and children. Listening and talking with our children is what we need to do, not talking to or talking at them.

Parents can negate the harmful effects of the sexualizing media messages and even counter the influence of friends by helping children develop critical thinking skills. As a parent, you may fear that by listening to their opinions and by encouraging them to question everything, you may have little anarchists running around in the house. But the fact is that while you may occasionally have heated discussions or long arguments with your teenaged child, these are not necessarily signs of a disconnected childhood. As long as moments of bonding and sharing with your child abound, which is likely to happen if your child feels you listen to him/her and are interested in his/her opinions, you have nothing to fear. Problems in relationships occur only when teenagers feel that they are never heard or understood by their parents—they can then either withdraw or fight all the time. More specifically, by not talking with your children about sex and sexuality, you are not preserving their innocence. Children will seek out information, whether the source is the Internet or friends, but then, the risk that such information will be incomplete, faulty or even harmful is quite high.

Approachability is another quality that can take you a long way in protecting children from harmful situations. Children of any age will approach a parent if they think that the parent will be open to hearing about their experience or answering their questions without being critical or judgmental. If you are open to talking to your child about any topic and have made it a habit to do so, your child is very likely to approach you when they want to discuss or make decisions on difficult topics, such as sex, drugs and alcohol. Being open to talking about different topics does not mean being permissive or even agreeing with the child's point of view. You may be perfectly comfortable answering any questions about sex in a factual manner but that does not mean that you give your teenage child permission to engage in early sexual activity. In fact, if you are comfortable answering these questions, you can as comfortably discuss the pros and cons of early sexual activity and let the child know your stance on this topic.

Being involved by taking an interest in your children's activities, their friends, their likes and dislikes, their music, their books, their thoughts and feelings, and not just their grades, will help them know that you care for them. Gone is the time when people could afford to be distant, aloof parents who loved their children immensely but would not show it except through enforcing strict discipline. No one, including children, can read your mind and assume that you care for them unless you show caring through your words and your actions. Words have to be backed up by action and vice versa—just one of the two also does not work.

So, go ahead and hug your teenager, even if he/she makes a face. Tell your children that you love them and tell them clearly what you expect from them, especially where sex and sexuality are concerned. Children are very resilient and many children who have faced enormous challenges, including child sexual abuse, have grown up to become healthy, happy adults. The one thing that has contributed to children's resilience without fail is the presence of a supportive adult in their life. So, go ahead and be that supportive adult in your child's life.

REFERENCES

Chapter 1: The Biological Underpinnings

1. Institute of Medicine (US) Committee on Understanding the Biology of Sex and Gender Differences; T.M. Wizemann and M.L. Pardue (eds). (2001). *Exploring the Biological Contributions to Human Health: Does Sex Matter?* Washington DC: National Academies Press (US), 3, 'Sex Begins in the Womb'; http://www.ncbi.nlm.nih.gov/books/NBK222286/.
2. Grayson M. Holmbeck. (1996). 'A Model of Family Relational Transformations During the Transition to Adolescence: Parent–Adolescent Conflict and Adaptation', in Julia A. Graber, Jeanne Brooks-Gunn, Anne C. Petersen (eds). *Transitions Through Adolescence. Interpersonal Domains and Contexts*, pp. 167–99. New Jersey: Lawrence Erlbaum Associates, Inc.
3. http://dictionary.cambridge.org/dictionary/english/puberty.
4. http://www.nimh.nih.gov/health/publications/the-teen-brain-still-under-construction/index.shtml.
5. Ibid.
6. http://www.health.harvard.edu/blog-extra/the-adolescent-brain-beyond-raging-hormones.
7. Ibid.
8. http://www.ncbi.nlm.nih.gov/pmc/articles/PMC3410522/.
9. Office of the Surgeon General (US); National Institute on Alcohol Abuse and Alcoholism (US); Substance Abuse and Mental Health Services Administration (US). 'The Surgeon General's Call to Action to Prevent and Reduce Underage Drinking'. Rockville (MD): Office of the Surgeon General (US). (2007). Section 2: 'Alcohol Use and Adolescent Development'; http://www.ncbi.nlm.nih.gov/booksNBK44366/
10. https://www.healthychildren.org/English/ages-stages/gradeschool/puberty/Pages/Physical-Development-of-School-Age-Children.aspx.

References

11. http://www.nhs.uk/Conditions/Puberty/Pages/Symptoms.aspx.
12. https://www.healthychildren.org/English/ages-stages/gradeschool/puberty/Pages/Physical-Development-of-School-Age-Children.aspx.
13. http://www.ncbi.nlm.nih.gov/pmc/articles/PMC3065309/.
14. http://www.nejm.org/doi/full/10.1056/nejmoa020880.
15. https://www.healthychildren.org/English/ages-stages/gradeschool/puberty/Pages/Physical-Development-of-School-Age-Children.aspx.
16. Ibid.
17. http://www2.aap.org/sections/endocrinology/precocious puberty.pdf.
18. http://www.mayoclinic.org/diseases-conditions/precocious-puberty/basics/risk-factors/con-20029745.
19. http://www.ncbi.nlm.nih.gov/pmc/articles/PMC3065309/.
20. Ibid.
21. http://www.mayoclinic.org/diseases-conditions/precocious-puberty/basics/risk-factors/con-20029745.
22. J. Mendle, E. Turkheimer and R.E. Emery. (2007). 'Detrimental Psychological Outcomes Associated with Early Pubertal Timing in Adolescent Girls'. *Developmental Review*, 27 (2): 151–71; http://doi.org/10.1016/j.dr.2006.11.001 http://www.ncbi.nlm.nih.gov/pmc/articles/PMC2927128/.
23. http://stayteen.org/myths.
24. http://www.gov.mb.ca/healthychild/mcad/growingupok.pdf.

Chapter 2: Touching Genitals: What is Normal and What is Not?

1. http://kidshealth.org/parent/growth/sexual_health/development.html.
2. www.Nctsn.org.
3. Ibid.
4. http://kidshealth.org/parent/growth/sexual_health/development.html.
5. Ibid.
6. http://psychologydictionary.org/masturbation.

7. http://www.nsvrc.org/sites/default/files/saam_2013_an-overview-of-healthy-childhood-sexual-development.pdf.
8. https://depts.washington.edu/hcsats/PDF/TF-%20CBT/pages/3%20Psychoeducation/Child%20Sexual%20Behaviors/Sexual%20Behavior%20and%20Children.pdf.
9. http://pediatriceducation.org/2013/08/26/what-are-common-sexual-behaviors-in-young-children/.
10. https://depts.washington.edu/hcsats/PDF/TF-%20CBT/pages/3%20Psychoeducation/Child%20Sexual%20Behaviors/Sexual%20Behavior%20and%20Children.pdf.
11. http://www.nctsn.org/sites/default/files/assets/pdfs/sexualdevelopmentandbehavior.pdf.
12. http://pediatriceducation.org/2013/08/26/what-are-common-sexual-behaviors-in-young-children/.
13. https://depts.washington.edu/hcsats/PDF/TF-%20CBT/pages/3%20Psychoeducation/Child%20Sexual%20Behaviors/Sexual%20Behavior%20and%20Children.pdf.
14. http://www.nctsn.org/sites/default/files/assets/pdfs/sexualdevelopmentandbehavior.pdf
15. Ibid.
16. https://depts.washington.edu/hcsats/PDF/TF-%20CBT/pages/3%20Psychoeducation/Child%20Sexual%20Behaviors/Sexual%20Behavior%20and%20Children.pdf.
17. Ibid.
18. http://pediatriceducation.org/2013/08/26/what-are-common-sexual-behaviors-in-young-children/.
19. http://www.nctsn.org/sites/default/files/assets/pdfs/sexualdevelopmentandbehavior.pdf.
20. http://pediatriceducation.org/2013/08/26/what-are-common-sexual-behaviors-in-young-children/.
21. https://depts.washington.edu/hcsats/PDF/TF-%20CBT/pages/3%20Psychoeducation/Child%20Sexual%20Behaviors/Sexual%20Behavior%20and%20Children.pdf.
22. Ibid.
23. Ibid.

24. http://www.apa.org/pi/families/resources/develop.pdf.
25. Ibid.
26. Institute of Medicine (US) Committee on Understanding the Biology of Sex and Gender Differences; T.M. Wizemann and M.L. Pardue (eds). (2001). *Exploring the Biological Contributions to Human Health: Does Sex Matter?* Washington DC: National Academies Press (US), 3, 'Sex Begins in the Womb'; http://www.ncbi.nlm.nih.gov/books/NBK222286/.
27. https://depts.washington.edu/hcsats/PDF/TF-%20CBT/pages/3%20Psychoeducation/Child%20Sexual%20Behaviors/Sexual%20Behavior%20and%20Children.pdf.
28. http://www.apa.org/pi/families/resources/develop.pdf.
29. R. Shashikumar, R.C. Das, H.R.A. Prabhu, K. Srivastava, P.S. Bhat, J. Prakash and P. Seema. (2012). 'A Cross-sectional Study of Factors Associated with Adolescent Sexual Activity'. *Indian Journal of Psychiatry*, 54 (2): 138–43; doi:10.4103/0019-5545.99532.
30. L.B. Finer (2007). 'Trends in Premarital Sex in the United States, 1954–2003'. *Public Health Reports*, 122 (1): 73.

Chapter 3: The Different Expressions of Gender and Sexuality

1. Just the Facts Coalition. (2008). *Just the Facts about Sexual Orientation and Youth: A Primer for Principals, Educators, and School Personnel.* Washington, DC: American Psychological Association; www.apa.org/pi/lgbc/publications/justthefacts.html.
2. Ibid.
3. Ibid.
4. B. Pickett. (2011). 'Homosexuality', in Edward N. Zalta (ed.), *The Stanford Encyclopedia of Philosophy* (Spring 2011 edition); http://plato.stanford.edu/archives/spr2011/entries/homosexuality/.
5. Gurvinder Kalra, Susham Gupta and Dinesh Bhugra. (2010). 'Sexual Variation in India: A View from the West'. Indian Journal of Psychiatry 52. Suppl.: S264–S268. PMC. Web. 4 January 2016.

6. K. Chakraborty and R.G. Thakurata. (2013). 'Indian Concepts on Sexuality'. *Indian Journal of Psychiatry*, 55 (Suppl. 2): S250–S255; doi:10.4103/0019-5545.105546.
7. Ibid.
8. Brent L. Bilodeau, Kristen A. Renn. (2005). 'Analysis of LGBT Identity Development Models and Implications for Practice'; https://www.msu.edu/~renn/BilodeauRennNDSS.pdf.
9. http://bisexual.org/qna/are-bisexuals-equally-attracted-to-both-men-and-women/.
10. Elizabeth M. Morgan. (2013). 'Contemporary Issues in Sexual Orientation and Identity Development in Emerging Adulthood', March, 1: 52–66; doi:10.1177/2167696812469187; http://www.apa.org/topics/lgbt/orientation.aspx.
11. Brent L. Bilodeau, Kristen A. Renn. (2005). 'Analysis of LGBT Identity Development Models and Implications for Practice'; https://www.msu.edu/~renn/BilodeauRennNDSS.pdf.
12. http://www.theguardian.com/commentisfree/2014/apr/17/india-transgender-laws-lbg-gay-communities.
13. K. Chakraborty and R.G. Thakurata. (2013). 'Indian Concepts on Sexuality'. *Indian Journal of Psychiatry*, 55 (Suppl. 2): S250–S255; doi:10.4103/0019-5545.105546.
14. http://www.apa.org/topics/lgbt/transgender.aspx.
15. http://www.apadivisions.org/division-44/resources/advocacy/transgender-children.pdf.
16. Ibid.
17. Ibid.
18. Ibid.
19. Ibid.
20. Ibid.
21. Ibid
22. http://www.apadivisions.org/division-44/resources/advocacy/transgender-adolescents.pdf.
23. http://www.apa.org/topics/lgbt/transgender.pdf.
24. http://www.gendercentre.org.au/resources/polare-archive/archived-articles/a-cross-dressing-perspective.htm.

25. Ibid.
26. http://www.apa.org/topics/lgbt/transgender.pdf.
27. http://www.theguardian.com/commentisfree/2014/apr/17/india-transgender-laws-lbg-gay-communities.
28. http://www.thehindu.com/todays-paper/tp-national/mother-seeks-groom-for-gay-son-matrimonial-ad-sparks-debate/article7228919.ece.
29. http://www.apa.org/topics/lgbt/orientation.aspx.
30. Gurvinder Kalra, Susham Gupta and Dinesh Bhugra. (2010). 'Sexual Variation in India: A View from the West'. *Indian Journal of Psychiatry*. 52. Suppl.: S264–S268. PMC. Web. 4 January 2016.
31. http://www.thehindu.com/todays-paper/tp-national/tp-tamilnadu/depression-stalks-lgbt-youth/article7142579.ece.
32. http://www.apadivisions.org/division-44/resources/advocacy/transgender-children.pdf.
33. Ibid.
34. http://www.apadivisions.org/division-44/resources/advocacy/transgender-adolescents.pdf.
35. Ibid.

Chapter 4: Pitfalls and Perils of the Internet

1. http://www.nimh.nih.gov/health/publications/the-teen-brain-still-under-construction/index.shtml.
2. http://www.internetsafety101.org.
3. http://www.nationalcac.org/images/pdfs/CALiO/impact-exposure-sexually-explicit-exploitative-materials.pdf.
4. 'Nevada Task Force on the Prevention of Sexual Abuse of Children Final Report'; http://dcfs.nv.gov/uploadedFiles/dcfsnvgov/content/Tips/Reports/SB258%20Report.pdf.
5. http://www.internetsafety101.org.
6. http://www.nationalcac.org/images/pdfs/CALiO/impact-exposure-sexually-explicit-exploitative-materials.pdf.
7. Jane D. Brown and Kelly L. L'Engle. (2009). 'X-Rated Sexual Attitudes and Behaviors Associated With U.S. Early Adolescents'

Exposure to Sexually Explicit Media'; *Communication Research*, Sage; http://crx.sagepub.com/content/36/1/129.abstract.
8. http://www.nationalcac.org/images/pdfs/CALiO/impact-exposure-sexually-explicit-exploitative-materials.pdf.
9. Ibid.
10. http://www.nbcnews.com/id/10912603/ns/dateline_nbc-to_catch_a_predator.
11. http://www.connectsafely.org/tips-for-dealing-with-teen-sexting/.
12. http://www.connectsafely.org/revenge-porn-is-about-betrayal-not-pornography/.
13. http://www.pewinternet.org/Reports/2009/Teens -and - Sexting.aspx.
14. Kaitlin Lounsbury, Kimberly J. Mitchell and David Finkelhor. (2011). 'The True Prevalence of "Sexting"'; http://www.unh.edu/ccrc/pdf/Sexting%20Fact%20Sheet%204_29_11.pdf.
15. http://www.rediff.com/news/2004/dec/15ekhan.htm.
16. http://www.rediff.com/news/2004/dec/17bazee.htm.
17. http://www.pewinternet.org/Reports/2009/Teens -and - Sexting.aspx.
18. http://www.dnaindia.com/lifestyle/report-cyberbullying-social-medias-darker-side-1712080.
19. http://www.fbi.gov/stats-services/publications/parent-guide.
20. http://www.endcyberbullying.org.
21. http://www.mcafee.com/in/about/news/2014/q2/20140603-01.aspx.

Chapter 5: Impact of a Highly Sexualized World: Hyper-sexuality and Body Image Concerns

1. http://www.pwc.in/en_IN/in/assets/pdfs/ficci-pwc-indian-entertainment-and-media-industry.pdf.
2. Munni Ray and Kana Ram Jat. (2010).'Effect of Electronic Media on Children', Department of Pediatrics, Advanced Pediatric Center, Postgraduate Institute of Medical Education and Research, Chandigarh; http://medind.nic.in/ibv/t10/i7/ibvt10i7p561.pdf.

3. J.D. Brown, K.L. L'Engle, C.J. Pardun, G. Guo, K. Kenneavy, C. Jackson. (2006). 'Sexy media matter: exposure to sexual content in music, movies, television, and magazines predicts black and white adolescents' sexual behavior'. *Pediatrics,* April, 117 (4):1018–27.
4. J.D. Brown, K.L. L'Engle, K. Kenneavy. (2006). 'The mass media are an important context for adolescents' sexual behavior'. *Journal of Adolescent Health,* March, 38 (3):186–92.
5. J.D. Brown, K.L. L'Engle, C.J. Pardun, G. Guo, K. Kenneavy, C. Jackson. (2006). 'Sexy media matter: exposure to sexual content in music, movies, television, and magazines predicts black and white adolescents' sexual behavior'. *Pediatrics,* April, 117 (4):1018–27.
6. J.D. Brown, K.L. L'Engle, C.T. Halpern. (2005). 'Mass media as a sexual super peer for early maturing girls'. *Journal of Adolescent Health*, May, 36 (5): 420–27.
7. Victor C. Strasburger. (2010). From the American Academy of Pediatrics Policy Statement, 'Sexuality, Contraception, and the Media'. The Council on Communications and Media, *Pediatrics*, 1 September, 126 (3): 576–82; doi: 10.1542/peds.2010-1544.
8. American Psychological Association. (2010). 'Task Force on the Sexualization of Girls'. Report of the APA Task Force on the Sexualization of Girls; http://www.apa.org/pi/women/programs/girls/report-full.pdf.
9. Carson A. Benowitz-Fredericks, Kaylor Garcia, , Meredith Massey, Brintha Vasagar, Dina L.G. Borzekowski. (2012). 'Body Image, Eating Disorders, and the Relationship to Adolescent Media Use'. *Pediatric Clinics of North America*, 59 (3).
10. 'Beauty and thinness messages in children's media: A content analysis'; http://jkthompson.myweb.usf.edu/articles/Beauty%20and%20Thinness%20Messages.PDF.
11. 'Beauty and thinness messages in children's media: A content analysis'; http://jkthompson.myweb.usf.edu/articles/Beauty%20and%20Thinness%20Messages.PDF.
12. From the American Academy of Pediatrics. (2009). 'Impact of Music, Music Lyrics, and Music Videos on Children and Youth

Council on Communications and Media', published online, 19 October, *Pediatrics*, 124 (5) 1 November: 1488–94; doi: 10.1542/peds.2009–2145.
13. P. Nieman. (2003). 'Impact of media use on children and youth'. *Paediatrics & Child Health*, 8 (5): 301–06.
14. From the American Academy of Pediatrics. (2009). 'Impact of Music, Music Lyrics, and Music Videos on Children and Youth Council on Communications and Media', published online, 19 October, *Pediatrics*, 124 (5) 1 November: 1488–94; doi: 10.1542/peds.2009–2145.
15. American Psychological Association. (2010). 'Task Force on the Sexualization of Girls'. Report of the APA Task Force on the Sexualization of Girls; http://www.apa.org/pi/women/programs/girls/report-full.pdf.
16. From the American Academy of Pediatrics. (2009). 'Impact of Music, Music Lyrics, and Music Videos on Children and Youth Council on Communications and Media', published online, 19 October, *Pediatrics*, 124 (5), 1 November: 1488–94; doi: 10.1542/peds.2009–2145.
17. Ibid.
18. S.C. Martino, R.L. Collins, M.N. Elliott, A. Strachman, D.E. Kanouse, S.H. Berry. (2006). 'Exposure to degrading versus nondegrading music lyrics and sexual behavior among youth'. *Pediatrics*, 118 (2); www.pediatrics.org/cgi/content/full/118/2/e430PEDIATRICS Vol. 118 No. 2 1 August 2006.
19. American Psychological Association. (2010). 'Task Force on the Sexualization of Girls'. Report of the APA Task Force on the Sexualization of Girls; http://www.apa.org/pi/women/programs/girls/report-full.pdf.
20. Ibid.
21. Ibid.
22. From the American Academy of Pediatrics. (2009). 'Impact of Music, Music Lyrics, and Music Videos on Children and Youth Council on Communications and Media', published online, 19 October, *Pediatrics*, 124 (5) 1 November: 1488–94; doi: 10.1542/peds.2009–2145.

23. Ibid.
24. K. Arya. (2004). 'Time spent on television viewing and its effect on changing values of school going children'. *Anthropologist*, 6: 269–71. Vivek Agarwal and Saranya Dhanasekaran. (2012). 'Harmful Effects of Media on Children and Adolescents', Review Article reported in *Journal of Indian Association for Child & Adolescent Mental Health*. 8 (2): 38–45.
25. http://unesdoc.unesco.org/images/0005/000595/059558eo.pdf.
26. P. Nieman. (2003). 'Impact of media use on children and youth'. *Paediatrics & Child Health*, 8 (5): 301–06.
27. Jane D. Brown, Kim Walsh-Childers, Cynthia S. Waszakb. 1990. 'Television and adolescent sexuality'. *Journal of Adolescent Health Care*. January, 11 (1): 62–70.
28. 'Beauty and thinness messages in children's media: A content analysis'; http://jkthompson.myweb.usf.edu/articles/Beauty%20 and%20Thinness%20Messages.PDF.
29. Ibid.
30. Victor C. Strasburger. (2010). From the American Academy of Pediatrics Policy Statement, 'Sexuality, Contraception, and the Media'. The Council on Communications and Media, *Pediatrics*, 1 September, 126 (3): 576–82; doi: 10.1542/peds.2010-1544.
31. Ross E. O'Hara, Frederick X. Gibbons, Meg Gerrard, Zhigang Li and James D. Sargent. (2012). 'Greater Exposure to Sexual Content in Popular Movies Predicts Earlier Sexual Debut and Increased Sexual Risk Taking'. *Psychological Science*, September, 23 (9): 984–93. Published online before print, 18 July 2012, doi: 10.1177/0956797611435529.
32. http://www.skprevention.ca/wp-content/uploads/2013/01/7-514-Sex-in-the-Media-Lit-Review.pdf.
33. Ibid.
34. American Psychological Association. (2010). 'Task Force on the Sexualization of Girls'. Report of the APA Task Force on the Sexualization of Girls; http://www.apa.org/pi/women/programs/girls/report-full.pdf.
35. http://www.skprevention.ca/wp-content/uploads/2013/01/7-514-Sex-in-the-Media-Lit-Review.pdf.

36. American Psychological Association. (2010). 'Task Force on the Sexualization of Girls'. Report of the APA Task Force on the Sexualization of Girls; http://www.apa.org/pi/women/programs/girls/report-full.pdf.
37. http://www.skprevention.ca/wp-content/uploads/2013/01/7-514-Sex-in-the-Media-Lit-Review.pdf.
38. American Psychological Association. (2010). 'Task Force on the Sexualization of Girls'. Report of the APA Task Force on the Sexualization of Girls; http://www.apa.org/pi/women/programs/girls/report-full.pdf.
39. http://www.skprevention.ca/wp-content/uploads/2013/01/7-514-Sex-in-the-Media-Lit-Review.pdf.
40. American Psychological Association. (2010). 'Task Force on the Sexualization of Girls'. Report of the APA Task Force on the Sexualization of Girls; http://www.apa.org/pi/women/programs/girls/report-full.pdf.
41. http://www.nationalcac.org/images/pdfs/CALiO/impact-exposure-sexually-explicit-exploitative-materials.pdf.
42. http://www.skprevention.ca/wp-content/uploads/2013/01/7-514-Sex-in-the-Media-Lit-Review.pdf.
43. http://www.nationalcac.org/images/pdfs/CALiO/impact-exposure-sexually-explicit-exploitative-materials.pdf.
44. Carson A. Benowitz-Fredericks, Kaylor Garcia, Meredith Massey, Brintha Vasagar, Dina L.G. Borzekowski. (2012). 'Body Image, Eating Disorders, and the Relationship to Adolescent Media Use'. *Pediatric Clinics of North America*, 59 (3).
45. Ibid.
46. Ibid.
47. http://www.mayoclinic.org/diseases-conditions/body-dysmorphic-disorder/basics/risk-factors/con-20029953.

Chapter 6: Child Sexual Abuse

1. http://wcd.nic.in/childabuse.pdf.
2. Mic Hunter. (1990). *Abused Boys. The Neglected Victims of Sexual Abuse*. New York: Fawcett Books.

3. L. Berliner and D.M. Elliot. (2002). 'Sexual Abuse of Children', in John E.B. Myers, Lucy Berliner, John Briere, C. Terry Hendrix, Carole Jenny, Theresa A. Reid (eds). *The APSAC Handbook of Child Maltreatment* (second edition; pp. 55–78). CA, Thousand Oaks: Sage Publications.
4. Mic Hunter. (1990). *Abused Boys. The Neglected Victims of Sexual Abuse.* New York: Fawcett Books.
5. L. Berliner and D.M. Elliot. (2002). 'Sexual Abuse of Children', in John E.B. Myers, Lucy Berliner, John Briere, C. Terry Hendrix, Carole Jenny, Theresa A. Reid (eds). *The APSAC Handbook of Child Maltreatment* (second edition; pp. 55–78). CA, Thousand Oaks: Sage Publications.
6. http://www.chicagocac.org/what-we-do/casacd/.
7. http://www.unwomen.org/~/media/headquarters/attachments/sections/library/publications/2013/10/voicesagainstviolence-handbook-en%20pdf.pdf.
8. https://www3.aifs.gov.au/cfca/publications/fathers-history-child-sexual-abuse-new-findings-f/export.
9. Danya Glaser. (2000). 'Child Sexual Abuse', *Principles of Medical Biology*, vol. 14, chapter 16, pp. 357–78. http://www.sciencedirect.com/science/article/pii/S1569258200800185;
10. Mark Chaffin, Elizabeth Letourneau and Jane F. Silovsky. (2002). 'Adults, Adolescents, and Children Who Sexually Abuse Children: A Developmental Perspective', in John E.B. Myers, Lucy Berliner, John Briere, C. Terry Hendrix, Carole Jenny, Theresa A. Reid (eds). *The APSAC Handbook of Child Maltreatment* (second edition; pp. 205–32). CA, Thousand Oaks: Sage Publications.
11. Mic Hunter. (1990). *Abused Boys. The Neglected Victims of Sexual Abuse.* New York: Fawcett Books
12. Mark Chaffin, Elizabeth Letourneau and Jane F. Silovsky. (2002). 'Adults, Adolescents, and Children Who Sexually Abuse Children: A Developmental Perspective', in John E.B. Myers, Lucy Berliner, John Briere, C. Terry Hendrix, Carole Jenny, Theresa A. Reid (eds). *The APSAC Handbook of Child Maltreatment* (second edition; pp. 205–32). CA, Thousand Oaks: Sage Publications.

13. Ibid.
14. Ibid.
15. Ibid.
16. Ibid
17. N.E. Latzman, J.L. Viljoen, M.J. Scalora, D. Ullman. (2011). 'Sexual Offending in Adolescence: A Comparison of Sibling Offenders and Nonsibling Offenders across Domains of Risk and Treatment Need', *Journal of Child Sexual Abuse*, 20 (3).
18. Ibid.
19. W.N. Freidrich. (2002). *Psychological Assessment of Sexually Abused Children and Their Families*. CA, Thousand Oaks: Sage Publications.
20. L. Berliner and D.M. Elliot. (2002). 'Sexual Abuse of Children', in John E.B. Myers, Lucy Berliner, John Briere, C. Terry Hendrix, Carole Jenny, Theresa A. Reid (eds). *The APSAC Handbook of Child Maltreatment* (second edition; pp. 55–78). CA, Thousand Oaks: Sage Publications.
21. http://nctsn.org/nctsn_assets/pdfs/caring/ChildSexualAbuseFactSheet.pdf.
22. Ibid.
23. L. Berliner and D.M. Elliot. (2002). 'Sexual Abuse of Children', in John E.B. Myers, Lucy Berliner, John Briere, C. Terry Hendrix, Carole Jenny, Theresa A. Reid (eds). *The APSAC Handbook of Child Maltreatment* (second edition; pp. 55–78). CA, Thousand Oaks: Sage Publications.
24. Carole Jenny. (2002). 'Medical Issues in Child Sexual Abuse', in John E.B. Myers, Lucy Berliner, John Briere, C. Terry Hendrix, Carole Jenny, Theresa A. Reid (eds). *The APSAC Handbook of Child Maltreatment* (second edition; pp. 235–47). CA, Thousand Oaks: Sage Publications.
25. L. Berliner and D.M. Elliot. (2002). 'Sexual Abuse of Children', in John E.B. Myers, Lucy Berliner, John Briere, C. Terry Hendrix, Carole Jenny, Theresa A. Reid (eds). *The APSAC Handbook of Child Maltreatment* (second edition; pp. 55–78). CA, Thousand Oaks: Sage Publications.

26. Debra B. Hecht, Mark Chaffin, Barbara L. Bonner, Karen Boyd Worley and Louanne Lawson. (2002). 'Treating Sexually Abused Adolescents', in John E.B. Myers, Lucy Berliner, John Briere, C. Terry Hendrix, Carole Jenny, Theresa A. Reid (eds), The APSAC Handbook of Child Maltreatment (second edition; pp. 159–74). CA, Thousand Oaks: Sage Publications.
27. http://cdn.basw.co.uk/upload/basw_103914-1.pdf.
28. https://www3.aifs.gov.au/cfca/publications/fathers-history-child-sexual-abuse-new-findings-f/export.
29. Vandita Dubey. (2006). 'A Qualitative Study of Resiliency Factors in Male Survivors of Child Sexual Abuse'. Chicago, IL; ISPP, Argosy University.
30. https://www3.aifs.gov.au/cfca/publications/fathers-history-child-sexual-abuse-new-findings-f/export.
31. http://nctsn.org/nctsn_assets/pdfs/caring/ChildSexualAbuseFactSheet.pdf.
32. Ibid.
33. Ibid.
34. http://www.stopitnow.org/ohc-content/what-you-can-do-before-a-child-is-harmed.
35. http://nctsn.org/nctsn_assets/pdfs/caring/ChildSexualAbuseFactSheet.pdf.
36. http://www.stopitnow.org/ohc-content/what-you-can-do-before-a-child-is-harmed.
37. Ibid.
38. Ibid.
39. http://sasian.org/sibling-sexual-abuse-a-parents-guide/.
40. http://nctsn.org/nctsn_assets/pdfs/caring/ChildSexualAbuseFactSheet.pdf.
41. L. Berliner and D.M. Elliot. (2002). 'Sexual Abuse of Children', in John E.B. Myers, Lucy Berliner, John Briere, C. Terry Hendrix, Carole Jenny, Theresa A. Reid (eds). *The APSAC Handbook of Child Maltreatment* (second edition; pp. 55–78). CA, Thousand Oaks: Sage Publications.
42. Vandita Dubey. (2006). 'A Qualitative Study of Resiliency Factors

In Male Survivors of Child Sexual Abuse'. Chicago, IL; ISPP, Argosy University.
43. Ibid.
44. Ibid.
45. http://www.stopitnow.org/ohc-content/what-you-can-do-before-a-child-is-harmed.
46. Vandita Dubey. (2006). 'A Qualitative Study of Resiliency Factors In Male Survivors of Child Sexual Abuse'. Chicago, IL; ISPP, Argosy University.

Chapter 7: What Parents Can Do

1. American Psychological Association, Task Force on the Sexualization of Girls. (2010). 'Report of the APA Task Force on the Sexualization of Girls'; http://www.apa.org/pi/women/programs/girls/report-full.pdf.
2. Ibid.
3. http://timesofindia.indiatimes.com/life-style/beauty/Delhi-teens-spend-a-fortune-on-cosmetics/articleshow/11093554.cms.
4. http://pediatrics.aappublications.org/content/early/2012/11/14/peds.2012-0095.abstract.
5. http://www.teenbodybuildingindia.com.
6. http://pediatrics.aappublications.org/content/104/2/341.full#sec-1.
7. E.W. Austin, B.E. Pinkleton, Y. Fujioka. (2000). 'The Role of Interpretation Processes and Parental Discussion in the Media's Effects on Adolescents' Use of Alcohol. *Pediatrics*. 105 (2).
8. http://pediatrics.aappublications.org/content/104/2/341.full#sec-1.
9. www.mediasmarts.ca.
10. http://www.skprevention.ca/wp-content/uploads/2013/01/7-514-Sex-in-the-Media-Lit-Review.pdf.
11. Rebecca L. Collins, Marc N. Elliott, Sandra H. Berry, David E. Kanouse, Dale Kunkel, Sarah B. Hunter, Angela Miu. (2004). 'Watching Sex on Television Predicts Adolescent Initiation of Sexual Behavior', *Pediatrics*, 1 September, 114 (3): e280–e89; doi: 10.1542/peds.2003-1065-L.

References

12. http://admis.hp.nic.in/himpol/Citizen/LawLib/C033.HTM.
13. http://www.trai.gov.in/writereaddata/userfiles/file/Cable_TV_Amendment_Act,_2011_final[1].pdf.
14. http://admis.hp.nic.in/himpol/Citizen/LawLib/C033.HTM.
15. Ibid.
16. https://www.aap.org/en-us/advocacy-and-policy/aap-health-initiatives/pages/media-and-children.aspx.
17. http://www.skprevention.ca/wp-content/uploads/2013/01/7-514-Sex-in-the-Media-Lit-Review.pdf.
18. https://www.commonsensemedia.org.
19. http://feministfrequency.com/2015/05/11/jade-beyond-good-evil/.
20. http://www.gamesforchange.org.
21. https://www.nationaleatingdisorders.org/50-ways-lose-3ds.
22. C.M. Wright, L. Parker, D. Lamont, A.W. Craft. (2001). 'Implications of childhood obesity for adult health: findings from thousand families cohort study', *The BMJ* (formerly the *British Medical Journal*), 1 December; 323 (7324): 1280–4; http://www.ncbi.nlm.nih.gov/pubmed/11731390/.
23. https://www.nationaleatingdisorders.org/50-ways-lose-3ds.
24. Ibid.
25. M.P. McCabe, L.A. Ricciardelli. (2004). 'Body image dissatisfaction among males across the lifespan: a review of past literature'. *BMC Public Health*, June, 56 (6): 675–85; http://www.ncbi.nlm.nih.gov/pubmed 15193964.
26. H. Al Sabbah, C.A. Vereecken, F.J. Elgar, T. Nansel, K. Aasvee, Z. Abdeen, K. Ojala, N. Ahluwalia, L. Maes. (2009). 'Body weight dissatisfaction and communication with parents among adolescents in 24 countries: international cross-sectional survey'. *BMC Public Health*, 6 February, 9: 52; doi: 10.1186/1471-2458-9-52. Also available at: http://www.ncbi.nlm.nih.gov/pubmed/19200369.
27. https://www.nationaleatingdisorders.org/50-ways-lose-3ds.
28. Ibid.
29. Ibid.

30. http://www.mirror-mirror.org/princess-diana-eating-disorder.htm.
31. D.N. Mendhekar, K. Arora, D. Lohia, A. Agarwal, R.C. Jiloha. (2009). 'Anorexia Nervosa: An Indian Perspective'. *National Medical Journal of India,* July–August, 22 (4): 181–82.
32. P. Mammen, S. Russell and P.S. Russell. (2007). 'Prevalence of Eating Disorders and Psychiatric Co-morbidity among Children and Adolescents'. *Indian Pediatrics,* 44: 357–59; http://indianpediatrics.net/may2007/may-357-359.htm. Ibid
33. A.A. Upadhyay, R. Mishra, D.N. Parchwani and P.B. Maheria. (2014). 'Prevalence and risk factors for eating disorders in Indian adolescent females'. *National Journal of Physiology, Pharmacy and Pharmacology,* 4 (2): 153–57; doi:10.5455/njppp.2014.4.041220131.
34. http://www.apa.org/pubs/info/brochures/girls.aspx.
35. Victor C. Strasburger. (2010). From the American Academy of Pediatrics Policy Statement, 'Sexuality, Contraception, and the Media'. The Council on Communications and Media, *Pediatrics,* 1 September, 126 (3): 576–82; doi: 10.1542/peds.2010-1544.
36. http://www.huffingtonpost.com/wray-herbert/the-perils-of-adolescence_b_6770678.html?ir=India.
37. http://womenofworth.in/dark-is-beautiful/.
38. http://www.thehindubusinessline.com/companies/advertising-standards-council-clamps-down-on-fairness-products/article6332424.ece.

Chapter 8: Investing in a Future Free of Sexual Violence

1. American Psychological Association, 'Task Force on the Sexualization of Girls'. (2010). 'Report of the APA Task Force on the Sexualization of Girls'; http://www.apa.org/pi/women/programs/girls/report-full.pdf.
2. Ibid.
3. http://idiva.com/photogallery-entertainment/bollywood-actresses-who-look-bad-in-bikini/31913/6.
4. http://www.unwomen.org/en/news/stories/2014/9/geena-davis-study-press-release.

References

5. http://www.unwomen.org/~/media/headquarters/attachments/sections/library/publications/2013/10/voicesagainstviolence-handbook-en%20pdf.pdf.
6. American Psychological Association, 'Task Force on the Sexualization of Girls'. (2010). 'Report of the APA Task Force on the Sexualization of Girls'; http://www.apa.org/pi/women/programs/girls/report-full.pdf.
7. http://www.asca.org.au/About/Resources/Impact-of-child-abuse.aspx.
8. http://www.antiviolenceproject.org/info/sexualized-harassment/.
9. American Psychological Association, 'Task Force on the Sexualization of Girls'. (2010). 'Report of the APA Task Force on the Sexualization of Girls'; http://www.apa.org/pi/women/programs/girls/report-full.pdf.
10. http://www.unwomen.org/~/media/headquarters/attachments/sections/library/publications/2013/10/voicesagainstviolence-handbook-en%20pdf.pdf.
11. http://www.aauw.org/article/pledge-to-let-the-girls-in-your-life-tinker/.
12. http://www.mavaindia.org/stories-of-change.html.
13. Ibid.
14. https://www.nationaleatingdisorders.org/50-ways-lose-3ds.
15. http://www.unwomen.org/~/media/headquarters/attachments/sections/library/publications/2013/10/voicesagainstviolence-handbook-en%20pdf.pdf.
16. http://www.skprevention.ca/wp-content/uploads/2013/01/7-514-Sex-in-the-Media-Lit-Review.pdf.
17. https://www.nationaleatingdisorders.org/50-ways-lose-3ds.
18. http://www.unwomen.org/~/media/headquarters/attachments/sections/library/publications/2013/10/voicesagainstviolence-handbook-en%20pdf.pdf.
19. http://www.livemint.com/Politics/llQdMpUC1fLMxKV04r2MCK/Genderbased-violence-is-an-epidemic-in-India-Kate-Gilmore.html.

20. https://www.nationaleatingdisorders.org/50-ways-lose-3ds.
21. http://www.livemint.com/Politics/llQdMpUC1fLMxKV04r2MCK/Genderbased-violence-is-an-epidemic-in-India-Kate-Gilmore.html.
22. https://www.nationaleatingdisorders.org/50-ways-lose-3ds.

ACKNOWLEDGEMENTS

Thank you, Dharini Bhaskar at Rupa Publications, for giving attention to this important topic and being considerate with timelines. Thank you to my family and friends for all the encouragement. Thank you to Shruti Tripathi, Annanya Mahajan, Aditi Dubey and Hritik Bhatnagar for their youth culture inputs. In Kumaon, thank you to Romola Butalia for the feedback and suggestions. Thank you also to Mohan Ji and Munni Ji of Satkhol Village for all forms of support, including the yummy food! Most importantly, thank you to all the amazing young people and families I have had the privilege of working with, and learning from, over the years.